Will Alsop book 1

this book is dedicated to Betty Alsop

Published 2001 by Laurence King Publishing
an imprint of Calmann & King Ltd
71 Great Russell Street
London WC1B 3BP
tel: +44 20 7430 8850
fax: + 44 20 7430 8880
e-mail: enquiries@calmann-king.co.uk
www.laurence-king.com

Distributed in the United States and Canada by
te Neues Publishing Company
16 West 22nd Street
New York, New York 10010
Tel: 212 627 9090
Fax: 212 627 9511
www.teneues.com

This book was designed and produced by Calmann & King Ltd

A catalogue record for this book is available from the British Library.

UK ISBN 1 85669 238 8
US ISBN 3-8238-5487-9

Text by Kenneth Powell
Captions by Will Alsop
Collaborator: artist Tim Thornton,
Illustrations on pages 204–5 by Nancy Alsop
Overleaf: Bruce McLean and Will Alsop in front of one of their painting collaborations

Printed in Singapore

Will Alsop book 1

Kenneth Powell

Laurence King

Light the first light of evening, as in a room
In which we rest and, for small reason, think
The world imagined is the ultimate good.
Wallace Stevens: *Final Soliloquy of the Interior Paramour*

Like the poetry of Wallace Stevens, the architecture of Will Alsop is a pure feat of the imagination. Stevens wished to discover what, in our secular age, poetry was. Alsop wishes, in spite of an age of secularised function, to make architecture. Both make art in which the sensuous and the cerebral are finely, almost painfully, balanced, but, in which, finally, the imagination is the only refuge. The outcome, beauty, is an act of faith, a testament that, amazingly, life is good and, with effort, has meaning.

Such language is seldom applied to contemporary building. Aesthetically, writers and architects are more preoccupied with battles of style; commercially, they struggle with the glib, misleading rhetoric of function. Trapped in the aftermath of modernism, they aspire to impose a purely external order where none exists. As a result, architects tend to 'discover' a mode from which 'design solutions' emerge like cloned rabbits from plastic top-hats. Confronted with virtual freedom, they draw the bars of a new, more efficient, more polite cage.

But, as Auden said, 'politeness and freedom are never enough/ Not for a life.' To live you need to be involved — therefore unfree — and ill-mannered. The ultimately inexplicable experience of beauty does not go down well at dinner parties and it certainly does not set you free. Rather, it makes awkward demands on your time and prompts you to say embarrassing things.

You are required to be exactly what Alsop is — a robust aesthete. There is nothing effete about his love of colour, form and space. It is immoderate, over the top. His buildings stop you in your tracks, demand your attention, just as the physical presence of the man himself inspires passionate, funny conviviality, long dinners and intense conversation. There is something to discuss here, something big. One day we'll work out what it is, but until we do, let's talk.

For Alsop does not build to live, he lives to build. His painting, especially in collaboration with Bruce McLean, his conversation, his humour, his family, his friends are all drawn into the process of design. He is not a professional for his life has none of the divisions of energy and attention that the term implies and, for the same reason, he is not an amateur. Rather he is a force that happens to express itself, all of itself, in buildings. As a result – from the swimming pool at Sheringham to the library at Peckham – encountering an Alsop building is exactly like encountering Alsop himself. One recognises them as a personality: complex, witty, jovial, playful, meditative and unresolved. I often find, when driving past Peckham, that I start talking to Will in my head.

Personality becomes, in his work, a solution to the failure of modernism to create a transmissable, public style. Others have responded to this failure either by embracing historical forms or mannerist functionalism – fair enough in their way – but only Alsop has had the sheer nerve to resort to this level of subjective conviction. From the start the risk was enormous. It still is, but less so because we have all grown more comfortable with the Alsop personality. That it works and that we have come to accept it is a testament to the power of the imagination – his and ours.

This is the ending of that great poem with which I began:
Out of this same light, out of the central mind,
We make a dwelling in the evening air,
In which being there together is enough.

Making a dwelling – calling something home – that is what architecture finally must do, in spite of everything, and that is what, in this extraordinary portfolio, it triumphantly does.

Englishness, beauty, imagination, colour, surprise, sculpture, consolation, comfort.

Brian Appleyard

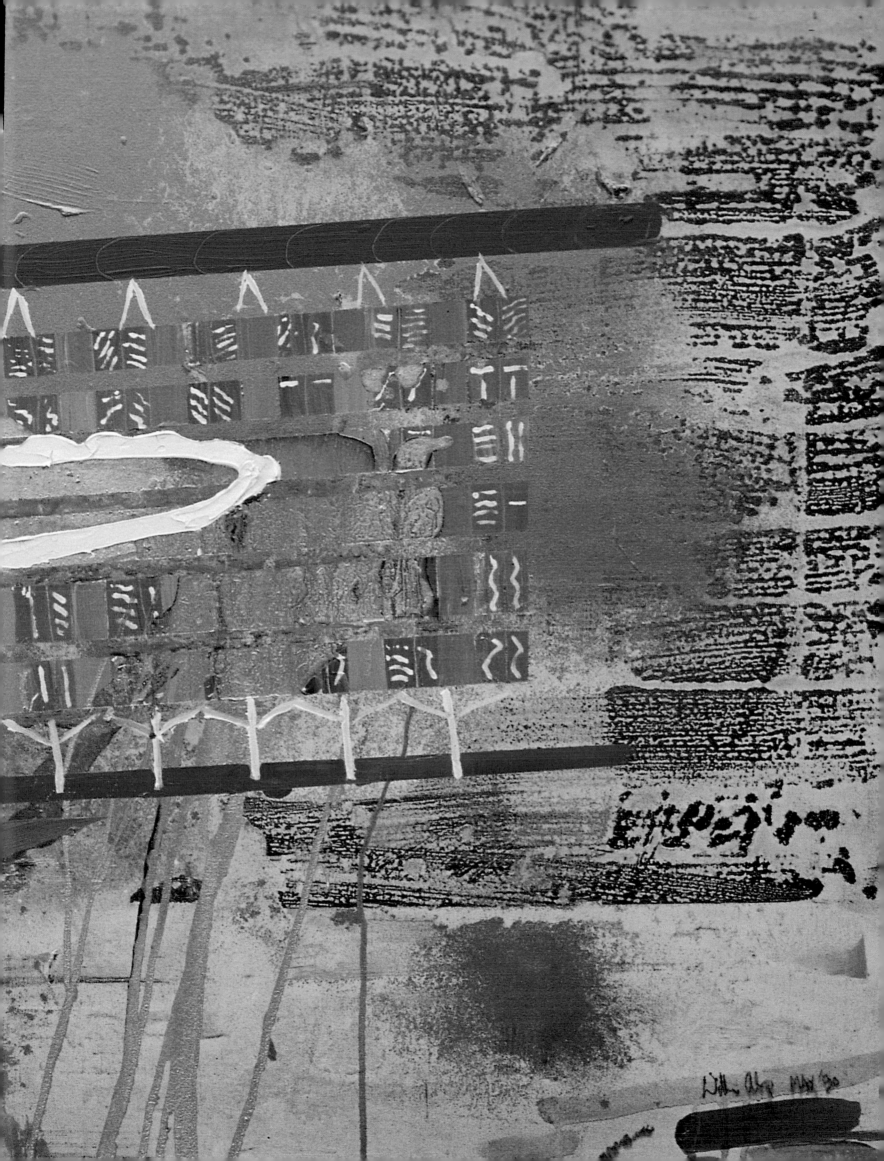

Previous pages:
L'Hôtel du
Département des
Bouches-du-Rhône,
Marseilles, 1990 –
an image made by
Alsop for the second
stage of the
competition.
(see page 157)

'The Flying
Bedstead': Alsop
believes this image
to be at the root of
English High-Tech
architecture.

A strange pose
articulates and
changes space:
Malcolm Pollard
– Alsop's tutor at
Northampton art
college – on a
Norfolk beach.

Alsop's father,
Frank (1885–1964),
and mother, Betty
(1912–1999), on a
picnic. Their love of
picnics always
influenced their

son's attitudes
towards
architecture and
permanence.

Alsop's bedroom in
Northampton, 1965.

suddenly, Northampton became a ghost town

8

Will Alsop was born in 1947, midway through the bleakest period of post-war austerity, in the middle of England. His birthplace, Northampton, retained something of the character of a county market town, though overlaid with the marks of nineteenth-century industry.

Charles Rennie Mackintosh worked there and Peter Behrens designed New Ways (1926), the first 'modern' house in Britain, for a local manufacturer – Alsop's childhood home was close to this pioneering icon. In more recent years, Northampton has become more closely linked to London – the growth of the new city of Milton Keynes from the 1960s irrevocably changed the character of this region of England. Back in the 1950s and early 1960s, however, the pace of life in Northampton was slow.

Before going to art school, Alsop took a job with a local architectural practice, where he learned to draw traditional details, to letter – and to make the tea. He recalls the gradual break-up of his circle of friends as, one by one, they drifted off to work or study, mainly in Birmingham or London – 'suddenly, Northampton became a ghost town'. Another melancholy landmark was the early death of his father in 1964, an event which marked another break with the past.

Though Alsop's later career has focused on cities – Hamburg, Marseilles, Vienna, for example,

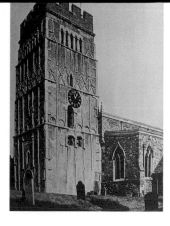

The understated
Saxon relief on
Earls Barton
Church,
Northamptonshire,
a building that
Alsop has admired
since childhood.

Wartime coastal
defences — an
architecture to
the point.

New Ways (1926) by
Peter Behrens — the
first modern house
in Northampton,
and one that Alsop's
mother hated.

Andrew Munro, a
fellow AA student
and co-founder
with Alsop of
MultiMatch.

This image of a
house by Ralph
Erskine excited
Alsop when he was
17 years old.

Rem Koolhaas (left)
at the AA in 1968.

A folding structure and musical instrument for the composer Harrison Birtwhistle, 1970.

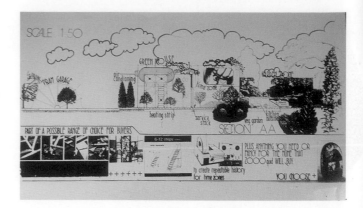

Alsop's design for a glass house won fourth prize in the Huddersfield Building Society design competition, 1971.

'Beauty Spot', 1969: a sensual game to be played in isolation.

we saw them as real proposals

Project Sink, 1970: a land-base prototype for a diving aid.

Simon Robinson — a friend from Northampton — collaborated with Alsop on a variety of art works. They held a joint exhibition at Compendium Gallery, Birmingham, in 1969.

Rural Guerilla

and, above all, London — his semi-rural roots show through from time to time. The English landscape and the classic English garden have been a constant influence. For some architects of an older generation — Richard Rogers, for instance — the countryside is an alien, rather disturbing place. For Alsop, in contrast, it seemed a place to be inhabited and enjoyed.

He once penned a science fiction novel on the theme of the Rural Guerilla — the idea of people surreptitiously inhabiting the countryside, avoiding the prohibitions of planning officers and eschewing the conventional charms of the country cottage, attracted Alsop.

Ideas of impermanence, the erosion of the gulf between town and country, the breakdown of established definitions of 'house' or 'building' and the abandonment of the programmatic functionalist agenda laid down by the Modern Movement have all figured periodically in Alsop's work over the last four decades.

By the time that Alsop entered the Architectural Association school in London (in 1968, a 'year of revolutions') the old modernist orthodoxies were looking shaky. The strong social and political programme which underpinned the school's teaching in the immediate post-war years was not yet entirely discredited — a version of it infused the work of

Wheeled feet allowed the structure to be moved when folded.

An experiment in folding lightweight structures carried out at the AA in 1969.

A dome designed to house an exhibition intended to create more awareness of the homelessness organisation, Shelter, at Tower Hill, London, 1969.

The dome under construction.

The 'Beauty Spot'
game.

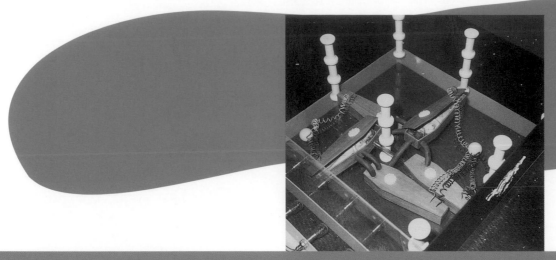

The door to the
diving capsule, part
of Project Sink,
1970.

Blickling Hall,
Norfolk – a
garden axis.

The eroticism of
high tech.

12

Project Sink evolved
into this (1970).

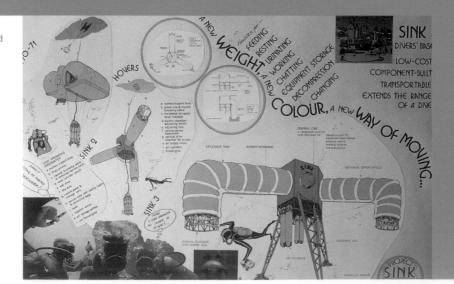

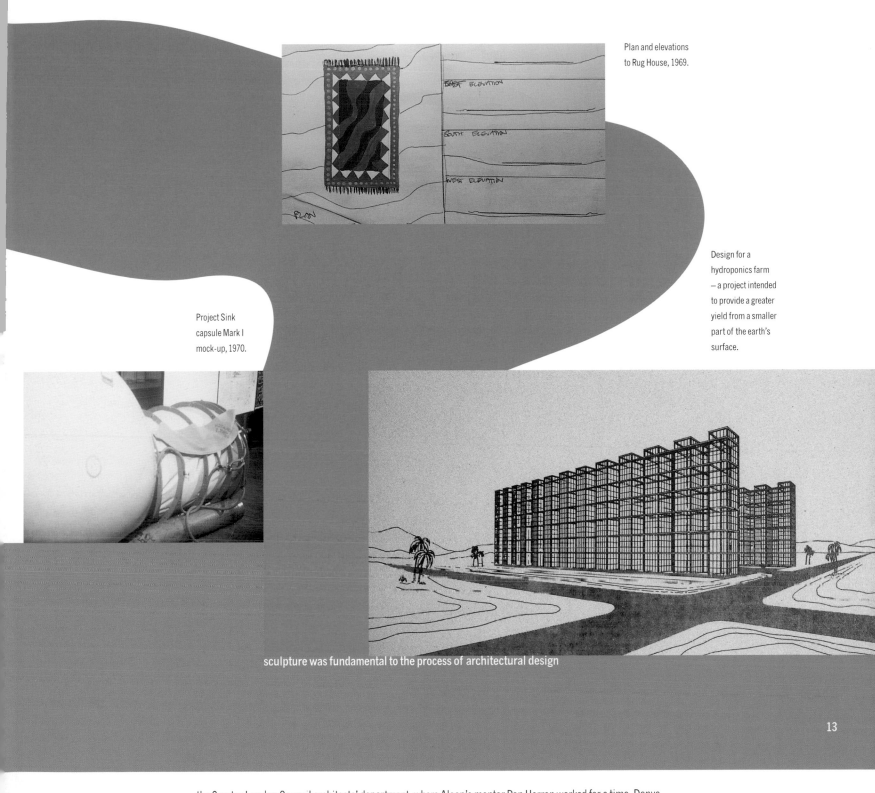

Plan and elevations
to Rug House, 1969.

Design for a
hydroponics farm
— a project intended
to provide a greater
yield from a smaller
part of the earth's
surface.

Project Sink
capsule Mark I
mock-up, 1970.

sculpture was fundamental to the process of architectural design

13

the Greater London Council architects' department, where Alsop's mentor Ron Herron worked for a time. Denys Lasdun was yet to build his National Theatre and work continued on the huge Barbican development in the City of London. The star of the commercial scene was Richard Seifert, though it was still unheard of for 'good' architects to work for property developers. Foster Associates had been established for just a year and was still desperate for work. The first major solo work of Richard Rogers was a retirement house for his parents. 'One of my visual icons at that time was the so-called "flying bedstead" — the first VTOL aircraft', Alsop recalls.

Will Alsop's own approach to architecture was coloured by the foundation year he had spent at the art college in Northampton. It convinced him that he did not want to make his living as an artist but also strengthened his conviction that painting and, more particularly, sculpture were fundamental to the process of architectural design.

(Alsop's use of painting as a first step towards the development of a project, an approach he has pursued since the mid-Eighties, is probably unique amongst major contemporary practitioners.) At Northampton, Alsop came to realise the importance of teaching through the example of some

Design for a house
of mesh and junk,
1972.

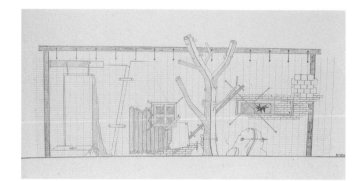

Virtual architecture:
waves on waves,
1971.

Flear Bed, an
exhibit in an art
show at Alexandra
Palace, London.
The bed concealed
bugging devices,
microphones and
amplifiers.

Warren Chalk, one
of Alsop's tutors at
the AA.

Pure anti-architecture

Mobility: Alsop has
always had a
fascination for
mobile shelters.

Dungeness, Kent
– a fascinating
landscape with
no apparent rules
related to aesthetic
control.

inspiring tutors – Malcolm Pollard, Henry Bird (who taught him to draw) and, above all, Osborne Robinson, well-known as a set designer. Alsop's early years of practice were combined, apparently seamlessly, with teaching sculpture at London's St Martin's school and it was possibly his strong sense of buildings as three-dimensional objects which made him resistant to the growing anti-architecture tendencies of the late Sixties.

'Aesthetics was a dirty word', says Alsop of his first impressions of the AA. 'It was a matter, it seemed, of taking the art out of architecture, of making it about problem-solving above all else'.

Le Corbusier, the dominant influence on British architecture during the 1950s, was now hardly mentioned, though Alsop revered his work. The influence of Archigram, the visionary think-tank which included amongst its members Dennis Crompton, David Greene, Warren Chalk, Ron Herron, Mike Webb and Peter Cook, was pervasive at the AA (then chaired by John Lloyd). One of Alsop's first teachers was Tony Dugdale, who had worked with Foster and Rogers at Team 4 and was 'a great teacher'.

This entry for the Centre Pompidou competition was awarded second prize in 1971. The project supposed that the majority of the space was underground.

Models for the Centre Pompidou competition.

Sheila Bean, Alsop's wife-to-be, in 1971.

Design for the Centre Pompidou competition.

House of Only
Privacy, 1971.

The impermanence
of land – plotting
the movement of
the North Norfolk
coast, 1971.

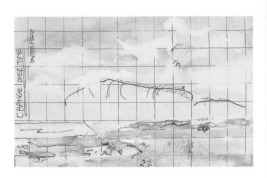

taking the art out of architecture

Decayed concrete: a
Norfolk aerodrome.

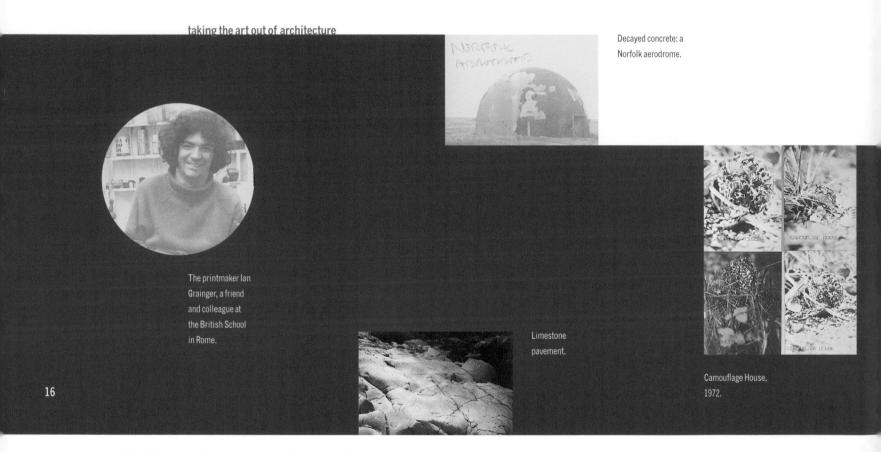

The printmaker Ian
Grainger, a friend
and colleague at
the British School
in Rome.

Limestone
pavement.

Camouflage House,
1972.

Keith Critchlow was an inspirational tutor in the geometry of structures. Robert Underwood taught pneumatics and
tensile structures, which were in favour as an aspect of the benign technology favoured at the time. A senior student,
four years ahead of Alsop, was Mike Davies, later responsible (as a director of Richard Rogers Partnership) for
London's Millennium Dome. (Alsop later recalled: 'we learned everything about tensile structures, domes,
pneumatics, etc, but virtually nil about concrete or steel!')

Rem Koolhaas entered the AA at the same time as Alsop. Although their architectural approach was to develop a certain affinity, leading to
mutual respect, they did not become close and Alsop's relationship with Koolhaas remains distant. Bernard Tschumi was someone with
whom Alsop enjoyed many stimulating conversations, finding his passionately radical views and advocacy of community action, 1968-
style, both surprising and exciting. Alsop's first-term project was a detailed survey of the Roundhouse in Camden Town, a former railway
locomotive shed then in use as a venue for rock music and experimental theatre.

Alsop was even then uncertain about the wisdom of 'taking the art out of architecture'. He persisted with his sculpture and had a show at
the Compendium gallery in Birmingham (see p.10). During the last term of the first year at the AA he worked with fellow student Andrew

Athens as a source
for a part of Paris,
1972.

Main square,
Heraklion, Crete,
1972.

Overleaf:
Maiden Castle,
Dorset, 1972.

Come And See

GEORGE & LITZA

MINOS K
MinoS

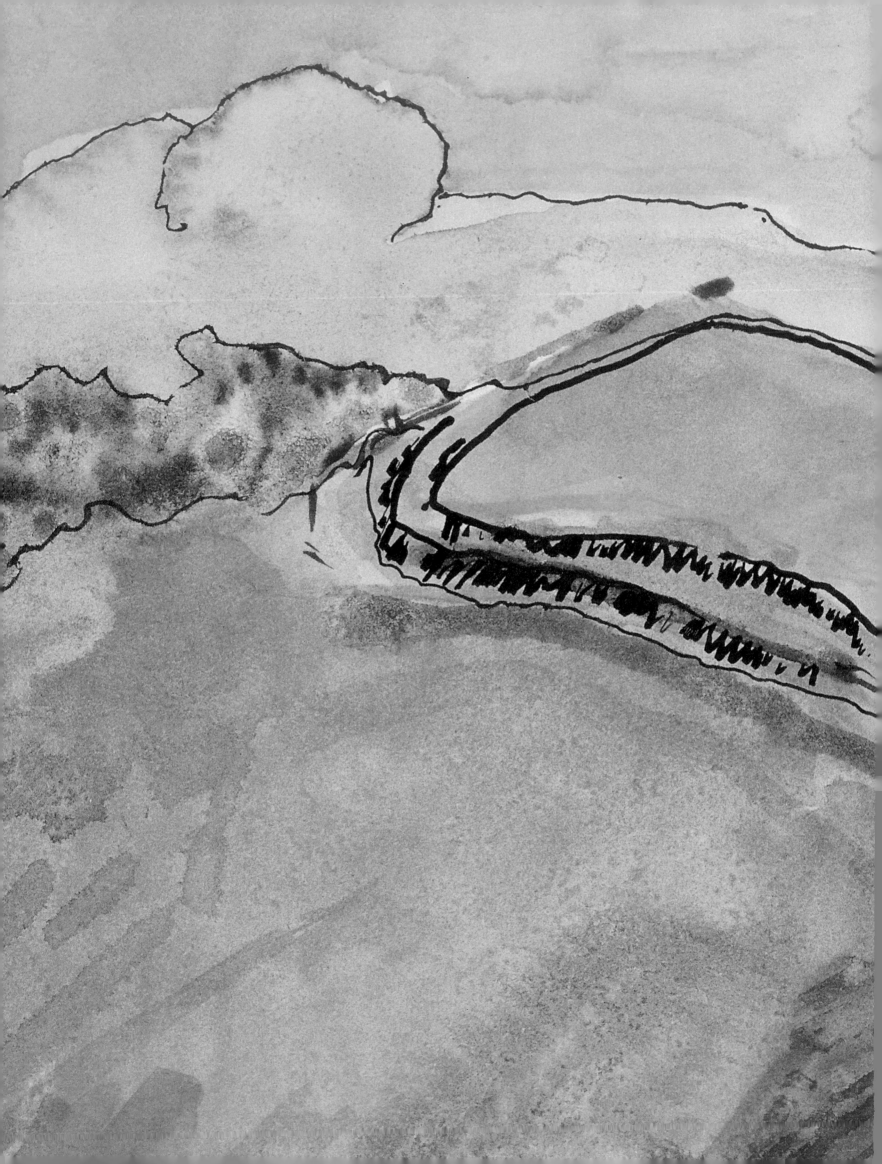

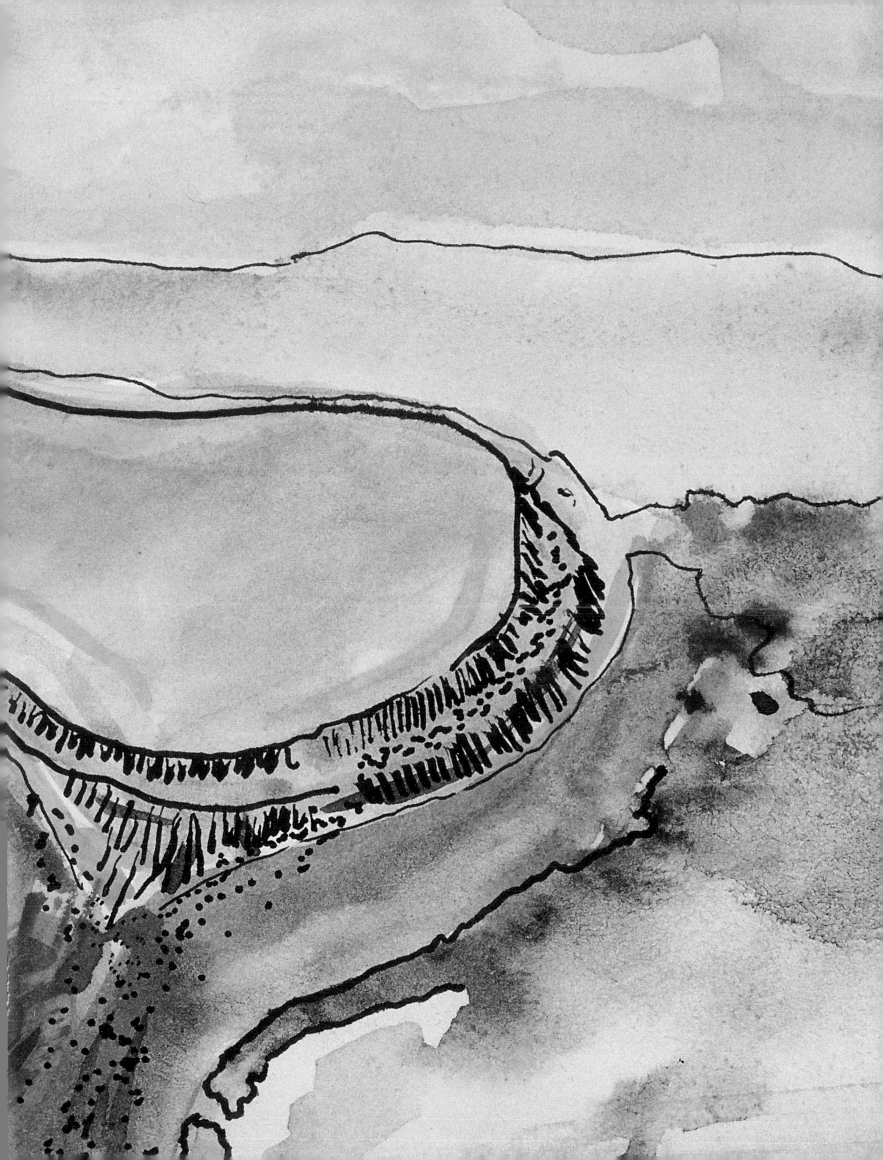

CLUE

A part of the great British Building.

I began to feel self-sufficient

Temporary installations in the Borghese Gardens, Rome, 1972.

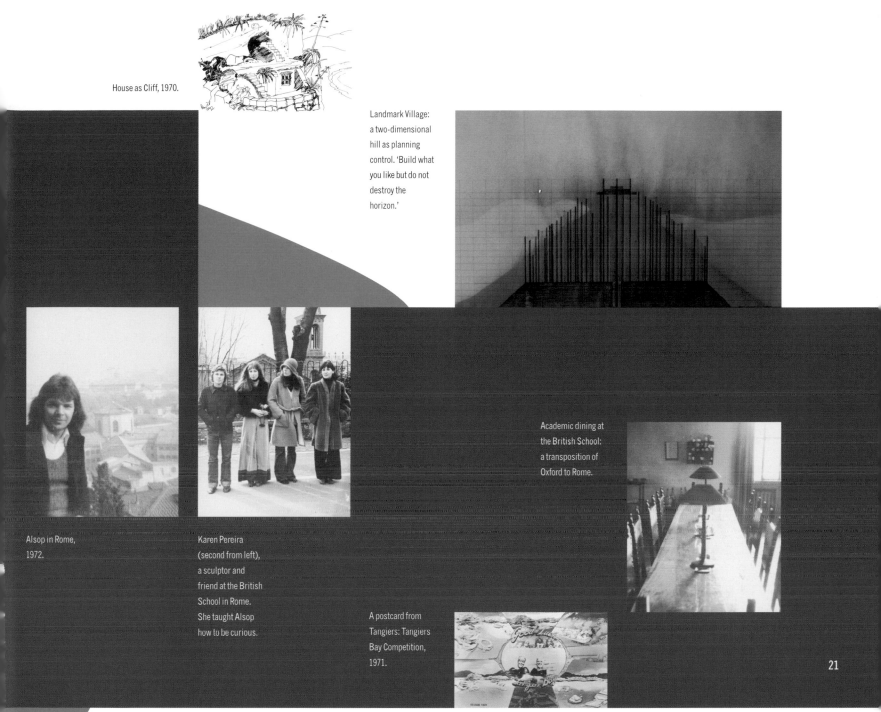

Overleaf:
A Light Concrete
Wall, 1972.

House as Cliff, 1970.

Landmark Village:
a two-dimensional
hill as planning
control. 'Build what
you like but do not
destroy the
horizon.'

Alsop in Rome,
1972.

Karen Pereira
(second from left),
a sculptor and
friend at the British
School in Rome.
She taught Alsop
how to be curious.

A postcard from
Tangiers: Tangiers
Bay Competition,
1971.

Academic dining at
the British School:
a transposition of
Oxford to Rome.

21

Munro on a mobile home project. There was also an installation for a performance of a new work by composer Harrison Birtwhistle and an exhibition for the charity Shelter (see pp.10–11). More significantly – the most important event of Alsop's life – working during the Easter vacation at Architects' Co-Partnership, he met his future wife, Sheila – they became inseparable and were married on 8th April, 1972.

It was during the second year at the AA that Alsop met John Lyall, the son of an architect from Southend in Essex, with whom he was later to form a professional partnership. Lyall seemed to share Alsop's conviction that narrowing architecture down to a technological agenda was a mistake – 'we were interested in lifestyle, ways of seeing, ways of living', Alsop recalls – 'human behaviour matters more than function'. Amongst the projects that Alsop and Lyall developed together in their second and third years was 'Sink 1' which focused – in remarkable detail – on the potential for underwater living (see pp.12–13). 'We did a lot of projects together', says Alsop, 'and we saw them as real proposals, not just vague ideas'.

It was during Alsop's fourth year at the AA, in 1971, as part of Warren Chalk and David Greene's unit, that he scored a

TO CHANGE THE WORLD, THINK ABOUT NOTHING

Landscape of
Recorded
Memories, 1973.

Minimal House:
white lines on the
landscape define
behaviour, 1972.

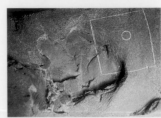

sometimes buildings simply get in the way

Alsop's bedroom in
Rome.

Façade of the
British School in
Rome by Edwin
Lutyens.

Mrs Alsop on the
island of Torcello,
Venice, 1973.

Alsop in the
Borghese Gardens,
Rome, 1973.

remarkable coup by coming second (to Richard Rogers and Renzo Piano) in the hotly contested competition for Paris's
Centre Georges Pompidou. Alsop's entry, designed with the help of fellow student Norah Cohen and with the advice of
David Greene, had to be submitted under the name of Dennis Crompton, one of the AA unit masters, since neither
Alsop nor Cohen was a qualified architect. If Rogers & Piano's winning scheme suggested the influence of Archigram
and of Cedric Price (who was subsequently to be such a key influence on Alsop), Alsop's proposal, for an undulating
landscape into which the various functions of the new centre were subsumed, reflected his conviction that landscape
matters as much as architecture – 'sometimes buildings simply get in the way'.

Alsop was proposing, in effect, a structure which had no obvious edges, which had an infinite
and unfinished look. Like Rogers & Piano, Alsop was convinced that the site, on the edge of
the densely built-up Marais quarter, needed to be opened up. Rogers & Piano devoted half of
it to a public square, which made their building, by Paris standards, quite tall. In Alsop's
scheme, 'the building itself became open space' – the facilities of the Centre would be
buried below the landscape (see p.15).

SLOW IT DOWN

More designs for Project Sink.

The Alsops and friend on a picnic in Kent.

David Gould, a painter and friend in Rome who loved Italy so much he married it.

The art historian Warren Tressider, a friend in Rome and an expert on Titian.

human behaviour matters more than function

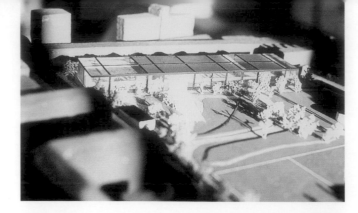

Early models for the Interaction Centre, Kentish Town, London (1973–7): this was Alsop's major work at the office of Cedric Price Architects.

Red Room work piece at St. Martin's School of Art, London. Alsop began teaching in the Sculpture Department in 1973.

Interaction brought home the disjunction between form and function

David Greene (far right) taught with Alsop at the AA from 1973 to 1975.

Landscape as architecture.

'I envisaged the Centre as two hills, with a central valley', says Alsop, who cites the Mappin Terraces at London Zoo as one of his inspirations. This extraordinary Edwardian structure was enjoying something of a vogue at the AA at this time, and Alsop's Pompidou project mirrored its combination of a concrete substructure with landscaping on top – at the Zoo, this was intended for bears. The Pompidou scheme was, says Alsop, 'pure anti-architecture – in a sense, it was avoiding the issue of a building, reflecting the mood that modern architecture was a disaster'.

There were echoes of Alsop's early preoccupations, in Rural Guerilla days, with the inhabited landscape and a hint of the famous Cedric Price adage that buildings in themselves rarely solve problems – it was Price who insisted that a client who came along asking for a new house might do better by getting a divorce and remaking his life.

Alsop quotes landscapes where architecture in a formal sense is an irrelevance – the City of the Dead in Cairo, a third the size of the inhabited areas of the city, or the Christiansland suburb of Copenhagen, run by hippies, with no rules, yet an agreeable place to live.

Evidence of the well-serviced landscape: an automatic water trough.

Flat pack home for a Rural Guerrilla.

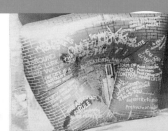

I had this idea of the impossible building, with no fixed function

Cedric Price on his fortieth birthday. Alsop joined his office in 1973 — the beginning of his second course in architecture.

EVENT

Pneumatic Wall for Graffiti manifesto and traffic piece, 1973.

NOT OBJECT

INTILLECTUAL
MORE
MAKE MO
HOMES
AROUND
LURK
WALLS
THE CITY IS A
CAPITALIST
GAMING INSTITUTE
SOCIETY ONLY CHANGES
THROUGH THOUGHT
AND ACTION
THE ARTIC
RULE
in the rich

...FULFILLED EXPECTATIONS
more freedom
means
CULTURED more police!
NDER GROUND
PROPERGATE

is this just
another
frances

YOU CAN

FORM OF POOR HOUSING
ROWD POOR WAGES
ONTROL POOR OPPORTUNITIES
MORE = POOR LIFE

mation MORE
is controlled
YOU landlords!
rite to
ressure on

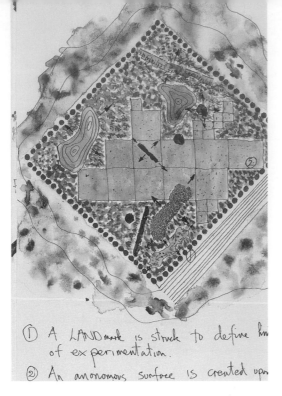

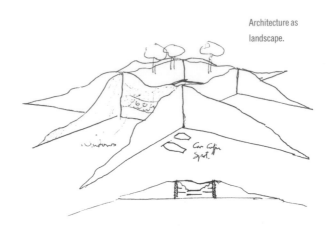

Architecture as landscape.

① A LANDmark is struck to define lim of experimentation.

② An anonomous surface is created up

Landscape of behaviour: a place to promote activity.

A piece of landscape granted architectural status.

Masterplan for
housing estate.

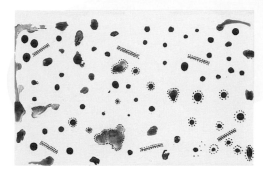

Masterplan for
housing estate.

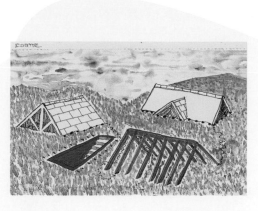

Landscape of
troglodites.

Overleaf:
Service building for
the beach, Spain,
1974.

A Rural Guerrilla,
1973.

landscape allowed me to exercise my desires to manipulate objects in space

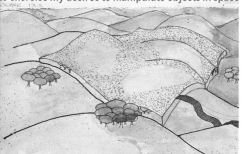

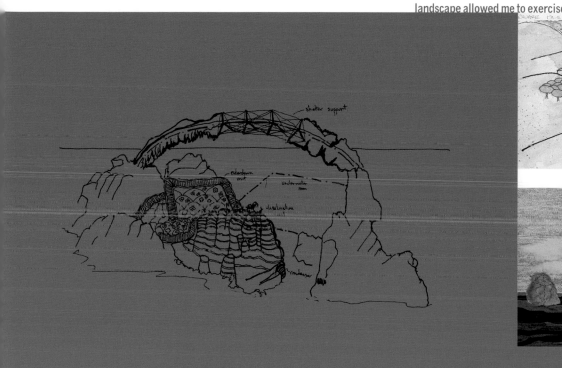

The ideas which circulated around the AA during Alsop's time there were those of a generation which questioned many hitherto unquestioned presumptions. 'Architecture without architects' was in vogue. The global triumph of modernism seemed to have produced disastrous results, so that vernacular and local ways of building were reappraised.

Only in 1973, with the Six Day war and resulting energy crisis, did 'green' issues really come to the fore, but there were already many proponents of alternative ways of living. Garbage housing was part of a trend towards recycling and eco-friendliness. The hippy movement which had surfaced in the mid-Sixties was part of the context of the time. Squatting, street farms and wind power were in vogue. Amongst the strands of radical thinking which emerged at this time was 'community architecture' – or 'people power' as some described it.

Alsop learned of the comprehensive development plans for London's Covent Garden from architect Brian Anson, then working for the GLC but later a pioneer of community action. He shared Anson's disgust at the proposals (subsequently defeated – a turning point in planning history) and was impressed by the dynamism and passion of the community activists. 'The people who live and work in an area should be consulted in the formation of a brief', he later wrote. 'However, the re-emergent use of the word 'community' encouraged the introduction of archaic fixed values into the area… Anyone would think it was the heart of the country'. Alsop looked to local communities not just to resist

THE ESTABLISHMENT OF RULES HAS BEEN THE DEATH OF ARCHITECTURE

Square Mile House,
part of the 'Five
Young Architects'
exhibition at ArtNet,
1975.

Landscape of
behaviour, 1974.

Rural Guerrilla
uniforms, 1974.

Garth Evans, a
sculptor and fellow
teacher on the Art
course at St
Martin's School
of Art.

Norman Willis, a
trade unionist with
a great interest in
architecture.

change but equally, where appropriate, to embrace it and to act as a catalyst for progress – the genesis of the C-Plex project in West Bromwich in the late Nineties exemplified Alsop's vision of a creative community architecture.

Whilst at the AA, Alsop, Lyall, Cohen and Munro had formed what amounted to a provisional architectural practice under the name MultiMatch – Czech students Jiri Skopek and Julius Tabacek also joined the team, as did Jim Monahan (himself to embrace the cause of community architecture and to play a leading role in the Covent Garden campaign).

MultiMatch established its own base, a mile or two from the AA, in a railway arch at Hungerford Lane, under Charing Cross station. MultiMatch was, Alsop now believes, part of the process of 'wiping the slate clean' and giving architecture a new start, jettisoning the functionalist agenda of the old Modern Movement. 'I want to underline the importance of the late Sixties and early Seventies as possibly the most important period in architecture', Alsop has written.
'I am aware that many consider it as rather a tired, dreary, end-of-an-era period, but the confusion, uncertainty and self-effacing nature of this period have contributed greatly to the culmination of the modernist period'… Preconceptions about the role of the architect and the purpose of architecture,

Elemental housing estate, 1975.

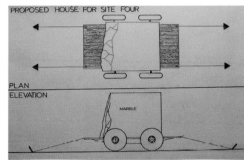

House designs based on clients' descriptions of a perfect day.

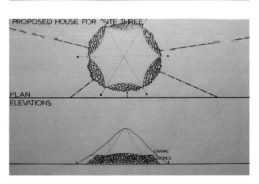

House design for Roderick Coyne, an artist and teaching colleague at St Martin's.

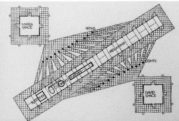

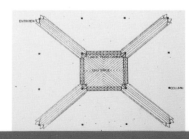

David Price, a colleague at Cedric Price Architects.

House design for the artist David Gould and his wife.

A house design for the journalist Stuart Mansell.

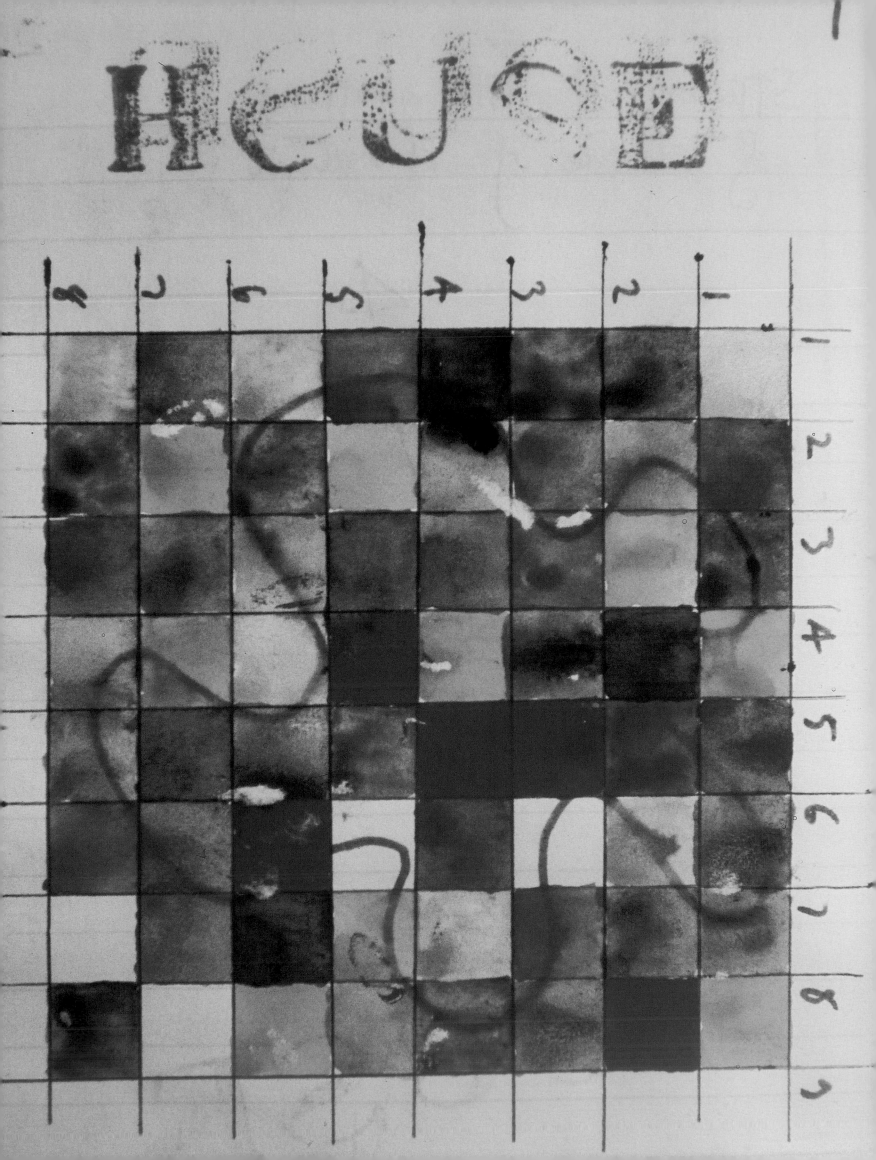

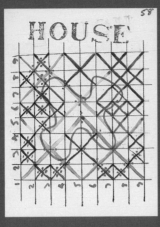
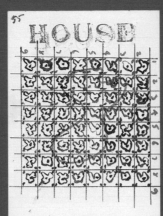

ALWAYS

DESIGN

SOMETHING

TO

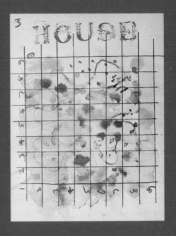

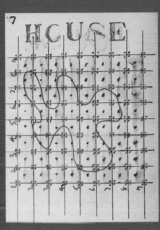
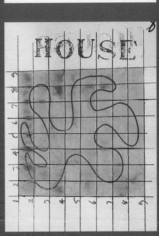
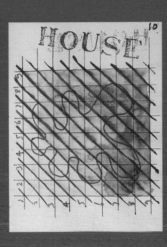

COMPARE

THE

DESIGN

TO

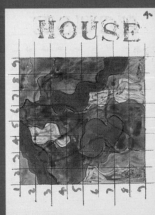

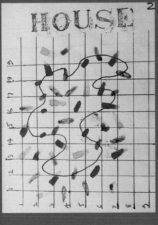
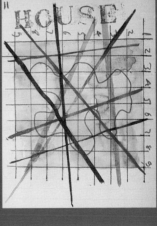

37

Pattern Book of
House Plans, 1975:
a potential rival to
the *Daily Mail Book
of House Plans*.

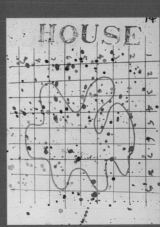

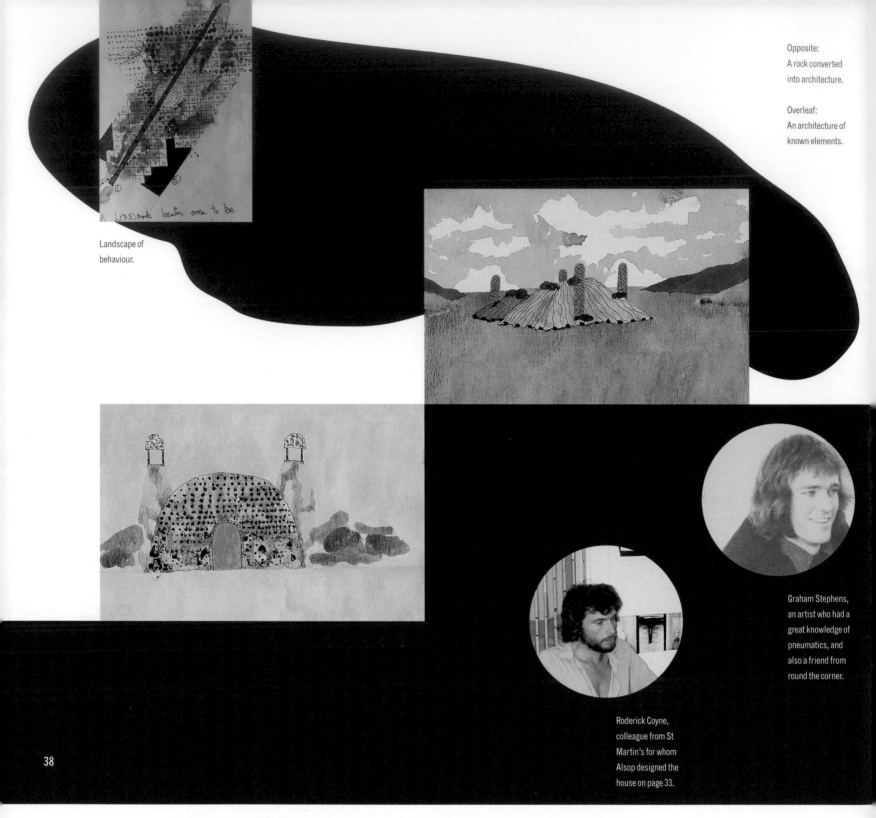

Landscape of
behaviour.

Opposite:
A rock converted
into architecture.

Overleaf:
An architecture of
known elements.

Graham Stephens,
an artist who had a
great knowledge of
pneumatics, and
also a friend from
round the corner.

Roderick Coyne,
colleague from St
Martin's for whom
Alsop designed the
house on page 33.

38

Alsop and his fellow conspirators believed, had to be completely abandoned and in particular the accepted dogmas about the hegemony of the architect were seen as obsolete.

While developing a firm conceptual and intellectual basis to his architecture, the young Alsop was also gaining practical experience. Unlike some of his AA contemporaries — one became an expert organ builder — he wanted to practise as an architect and to create buildings. Instead of taking a 'year out' working in a practice for his fourth year — as was usual — he combined study at the school with part-time work for several offices. One of them was that of Maxwell Fry and Jane Drew, esteemed modernists of the older generation who had established their reputations before the Second World War.

Alsop admired their work, especially the sculptural, Ronchamp-inspired crematorium near Bridgend, South Wales, and warmed to their interest in the arts — Eduardo Paolozzi was a close friend who lodged with Fry and Drew for a time. Alsop drove himself hard that year, entering competitions — he came fourth in one organised by the Huddersfield Building Society to design new housing (see p.10).

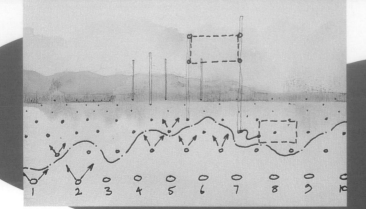

A well-serviced
landscape.

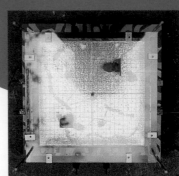

Model of one room
for a house with six
identical rooms.
Each room
contained
everything a whole
house requires:
toilet, cooker,
shower, etc.

John Jenner, a
colleague at Cedric
Price Architects.

Garth Evans,
a friend.

Alsop travelling on
a train through
Battersea on his
way to Japan, 1975.

42

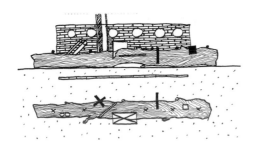

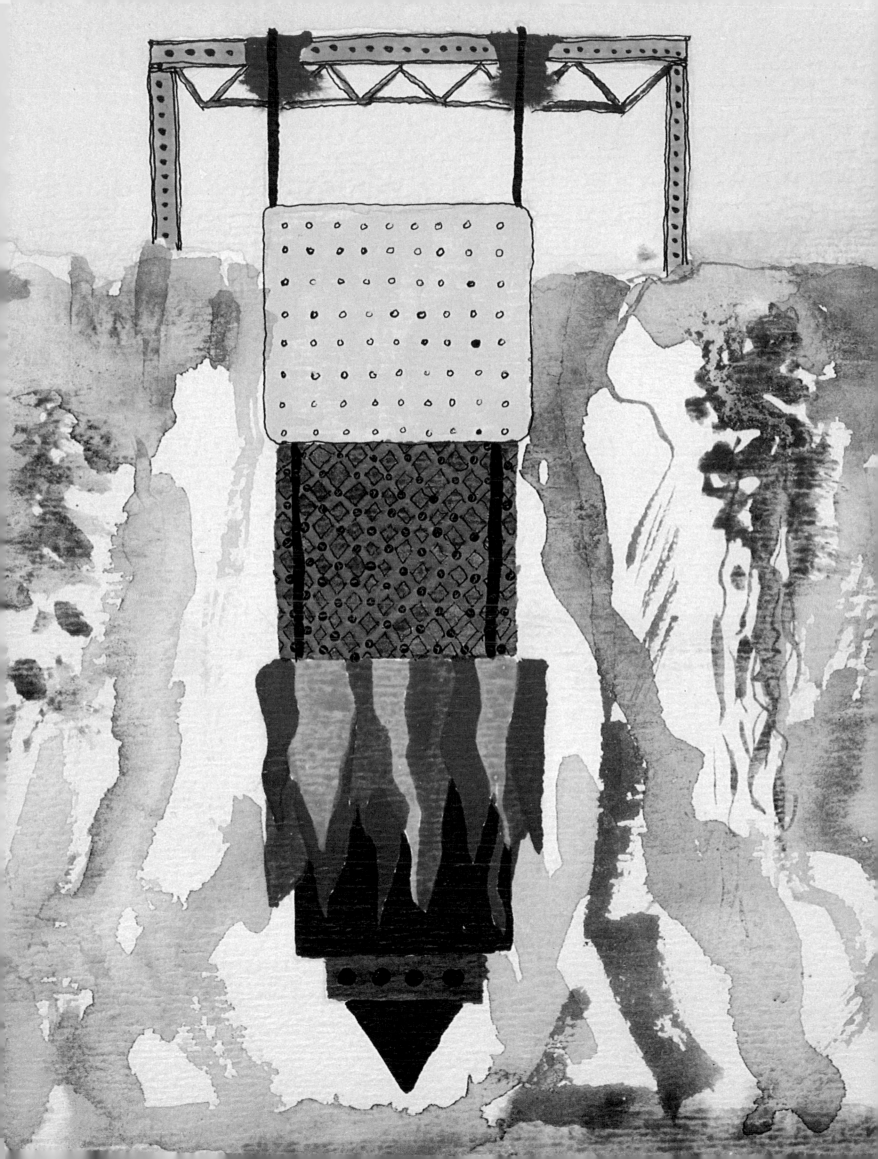

Signs on water
denoting the
presence of
architecture.

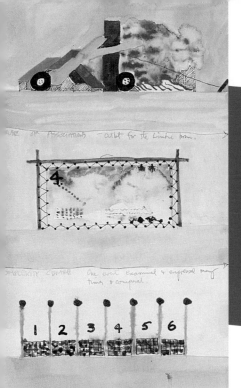

Selected pages
from a masterplan
for a town of
assorted possible
behaviour centres.

DESIGN
A
RANGE
OF
OBJECTS
THAT
CANNOT
BE
RELATED
TO
THEIR
NAME

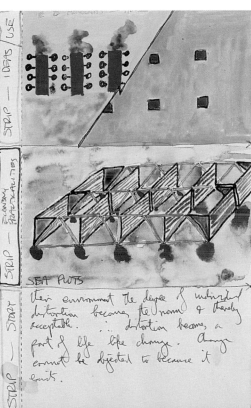

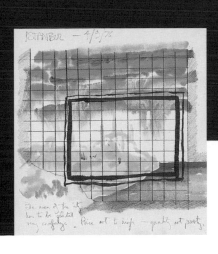

NO DEFINITIONS

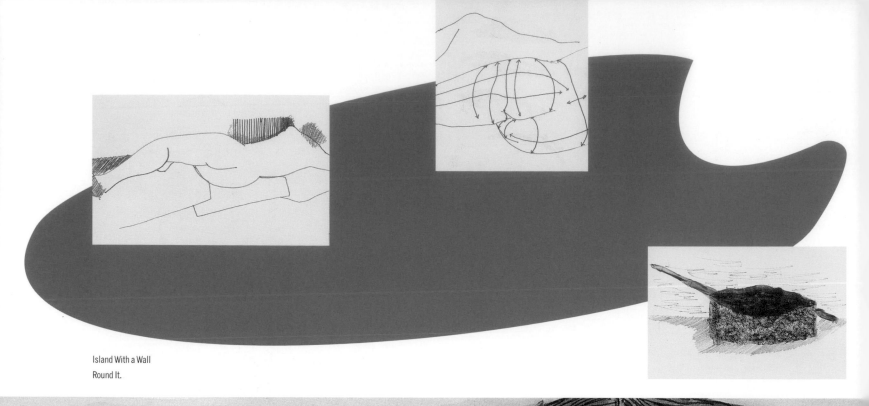

Island With a Wall
Round It.

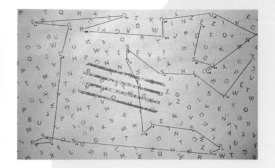

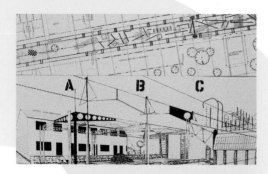

Proposals for
housing renewal
strategies for
Leuven, Belgium.

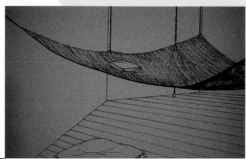

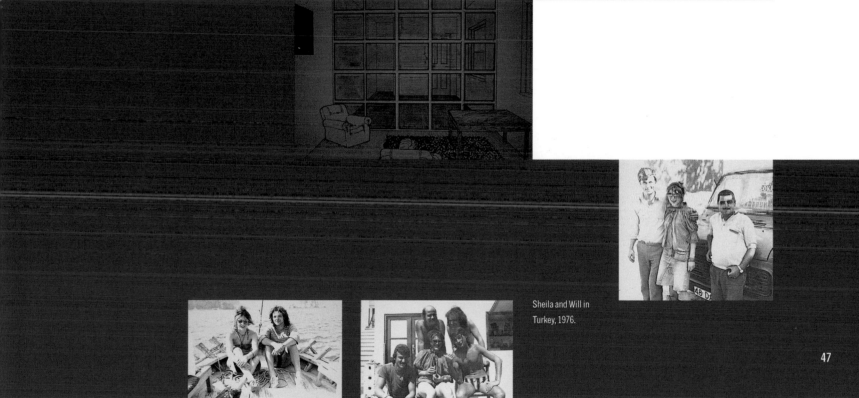

Sheila and Will in
Turkey, 1976.

Alsop's AA career culminated in a well-earned scholarship to the British School in Rome which he
was allowed to combine with his fifth year studies. 'I was nominally in Peter Cook's unit', he says,
'but we hardly met!' It was a hugely rewarding experience, Alsop recalls (see pp.20–21, 24–5).

Intense bouts of drawing were followed by evenings dining out, going to the cinema, or simply
talking to fellow students — writers and artists, with whom Alsop got on well. (He particularly
recalls poet Paul Aston, printmaker Ian Grainger and sculptor Karen Pereira.)

The year in Rome, says Alsop, was one of transition: 'I began to feel self-sufficient — an individual, not just a member
of a class or unit. After all, I'd hardly been abroad at the time, let alone lived abroad for any length of time, though a
holiday in Greece had opened my eyes to the Mediterranean culture. Like everyone from northern Europe, I was
entranced by the light'. Alsop's new self-confidence was reflected in his competition scheme, submitted from Rome,
for the County Hall in his home town of Northampton. Alsop's entry was rooted in a view of landscape and drew some
inspiration from Maiden Castle in Dorset (see pp.18–19). The competition was won by Jeremy & Fenella Dixon, but the
project was subsequently abandoned.

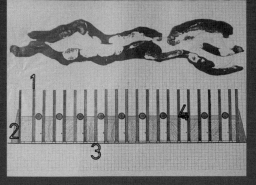

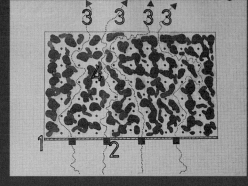

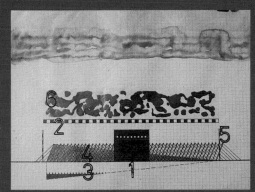

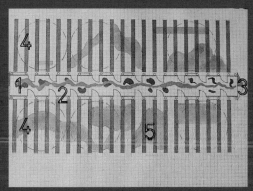

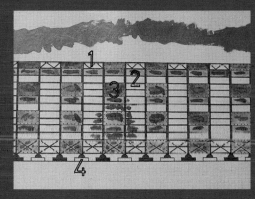

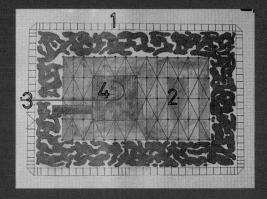

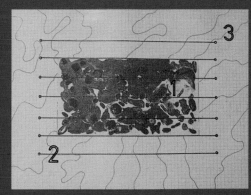

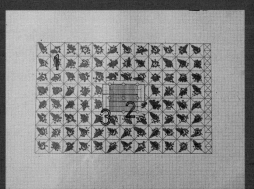

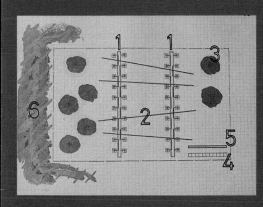

49

MY WORK IS CONNECTED TO THE QUESTION OF

Interaction Centre,
Kentish Town,
London, in various
stages of unfinish,
1977.

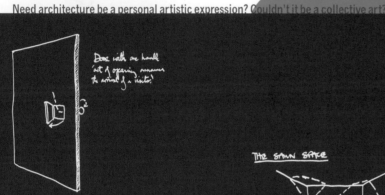

Need architecture be a personal artistic expression? Couldn't it be a collective art?

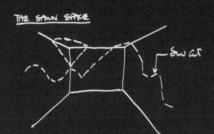

50

'I could hardly claim that the architecture of Rome greatly influenced my own approach to design', says Alsop. 'I loved the views, like that from the Borghese Gardens, and the landscape of Rome more than the buildings, though the grave simplicity of the Pantheon and the way that the Baths of Caracalla were 'inhabited' by a number of uses, for example, as an outdoor stage, did strike me, as did the great sense of space in the major monuments.

It was probably the climate, the lifestyle, the food, the wine that really hit me — as it did anyone brought up in austere 1950s England'. The way that life flowed through ancient sites and monuments impressed Alsop. 'I had this vision of the impossible building, with no fixed function, totally non-prescriptive, not designed to programme people but to let them thrive'.

THE REMOVAL OF DISAPPOINTMENT

On his return from Rome in the summer of 1973, Alsop secured a post in a far from conventional architectural practice — as a newly married man, he needed to earn a living, but instinctively avoided mainline practices . 'I spent three years trying to understand him', says Alsop of Cedric Price in whose office he spent five highly significant years after leaving the AA. 'Working for him was like enrolling in a second

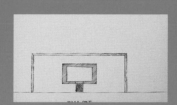

A proposal for a series of walls around a decaying house that would record the location

of the original work, featuring edges, cornices, windows, and so on.

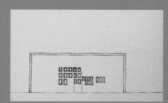

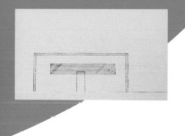

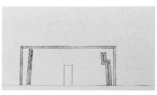

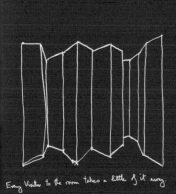

Every Visitor to the room takes a little of it away.

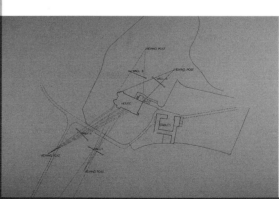

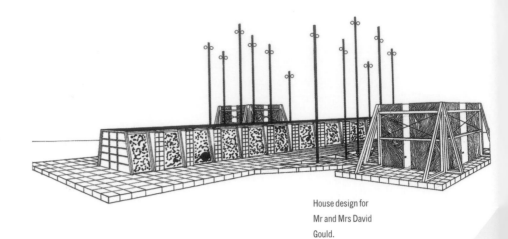

House design for
Mr and Mrs David
Gould.

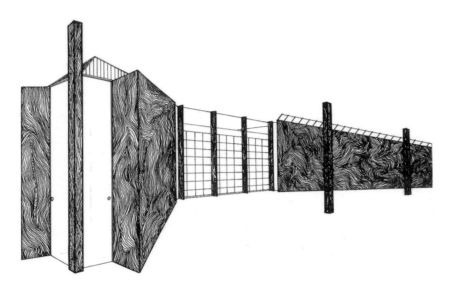

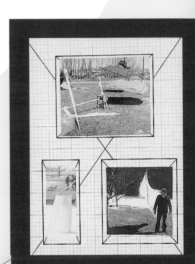

House design for
June Collier.

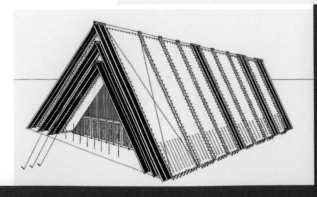

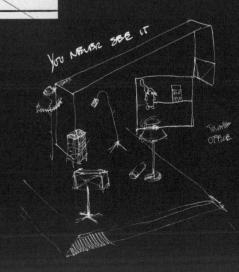

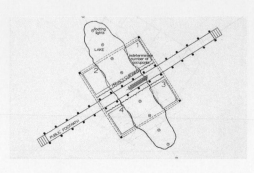

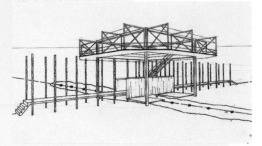

House design for
Ken Adams.

Overleaf:
Landscape filters.

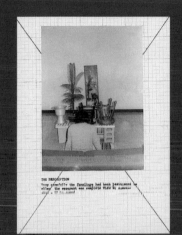

Exercises in
creating physical
narrative at Ball
State University,
Indiana, 1977.

SMALL SKYSCRAPERS
reduced scale
what's effect?

course in architecture'. Price is one of the best-known, most respected, yet least understood, figures on the British architectural scene. Alsop says of Price: 'The first thing that attracted me to Cedric was his Englishness. I consider that eloquence has always been of prime importance to the English…

Understatement has always been a quality of the British and Cedric, in his built work, is a prime example'. Alsop characterises Price as someone whose built work (and it is small in extent) can be separated from his role as an observer and critic, bent on creating a new way of building to serve the needs of the process of social transformation to which Price is genuinely committed.

Soon after Alsop's arrival in the Price atelier, Cedric Price began work on a project which epitomised his philosophy of design: the Interaction studio complex in London's Kentish Town. The clients (with whom Alsop was deputed to deal) were a diverse body of artists and arts enthusiasts. They had secured the confined site, close to a railway line, from Camden Council. The lease was short and the buildings had to be cheap — the budget seemed to gradually diminish! — and impermanent, as well as flexible. 'Cedric welcomed this', says Alsop, 'and for me Interaction brought home the

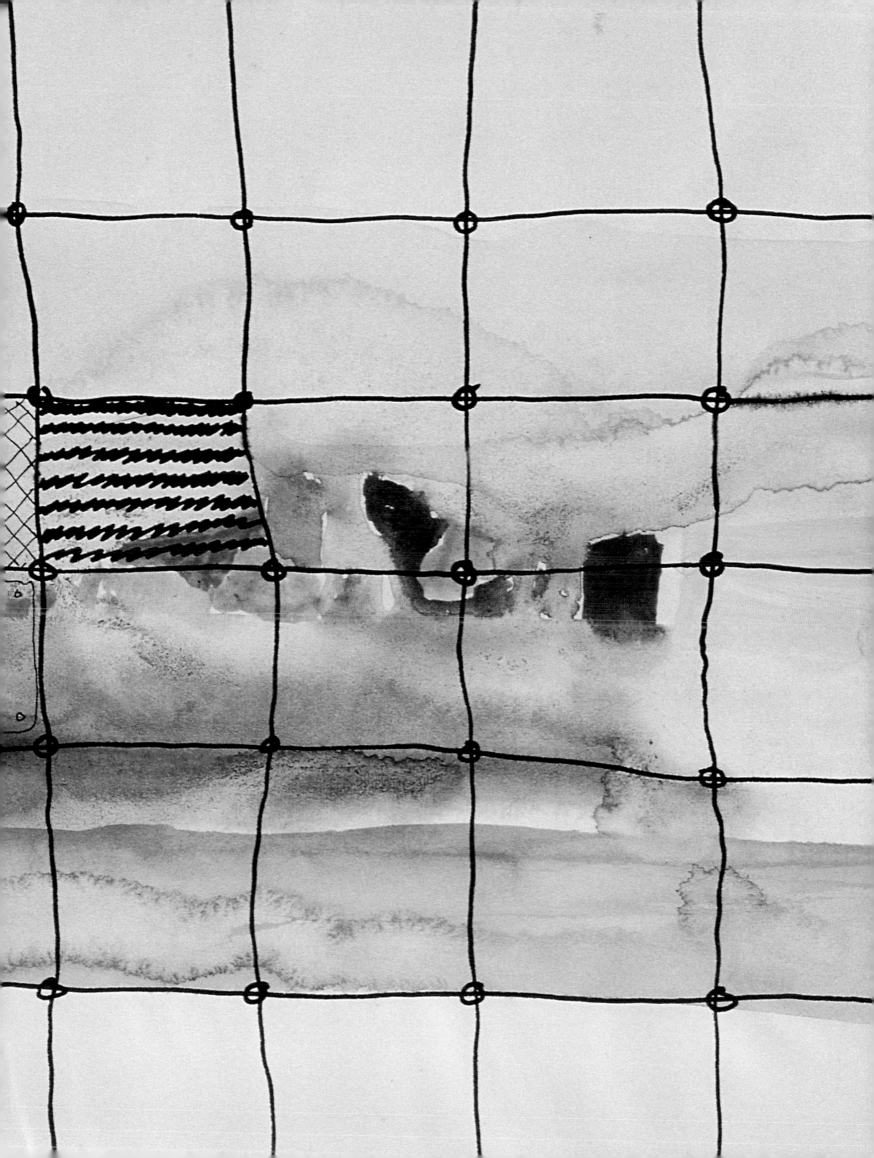

The campus at Ball
State University –
architectural
banality.

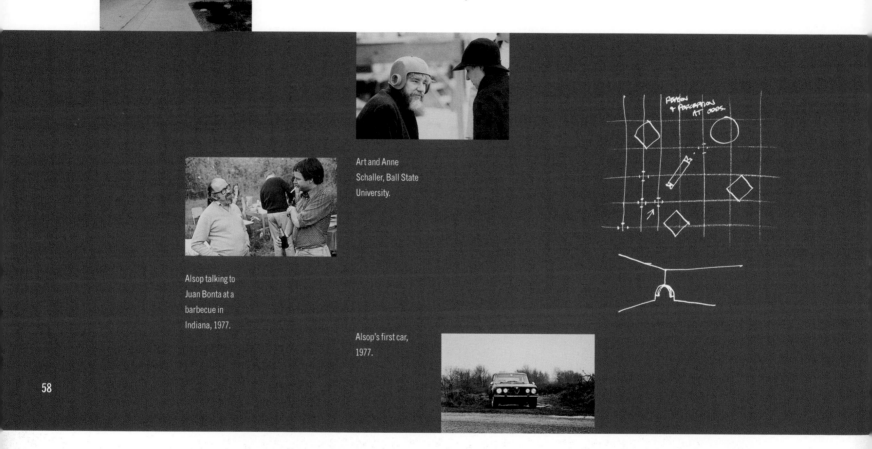

Art and Anne
Schaller, Ball State
University.

Alsop talking to
Juan Bonta at a
barbecue in
Indiana, 1977.

Alsop's first car,
1977.

58

disjunction between form and function' (see p.50). There was a power supply to the site. Drainage had to be installed.
Apart from that, there was money only for a concrete slab and for a steel frame in which studio units would be installed
as and when funding allowed. Interaction was virtually designed on site – it was a matter of 'drawing on the concrete
slab', says Alsop, and there was a tremendous feeling of involvement and ownership. After four years, Interaction was
virtually complete and the end of the project coincided neatly with Alsop's departure from the office.

Price's famous indifference to aesthetics was matched by his distaste for structural gymnastics – engineering, he
insisted, was a means to an end, not something to be celebrated in its own right. (Price, in fact, collaborated with the
engineer Frank Newby on many occasions – it was a partnership of equals.)

Amongst the projects on which Alsop worked during his time with Price were the proposed floating breakwater for
Abu Dhabi and the research for contractor McAlpine into site safety. Studying the design of workers' clothing and
the nature of site catering arrangements interested Price greatly – architecture was part of a broad spectrum of
human life which he saw as his proper concern.

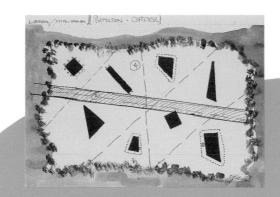

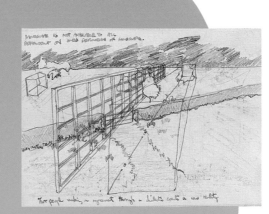

The name of the
home determines
the form.

59

Paul Shepheard, co-
founder with Alsop
of the London
Architecture Club.

Sheila Alsop
working at the AA.

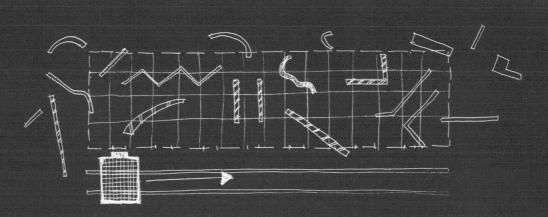

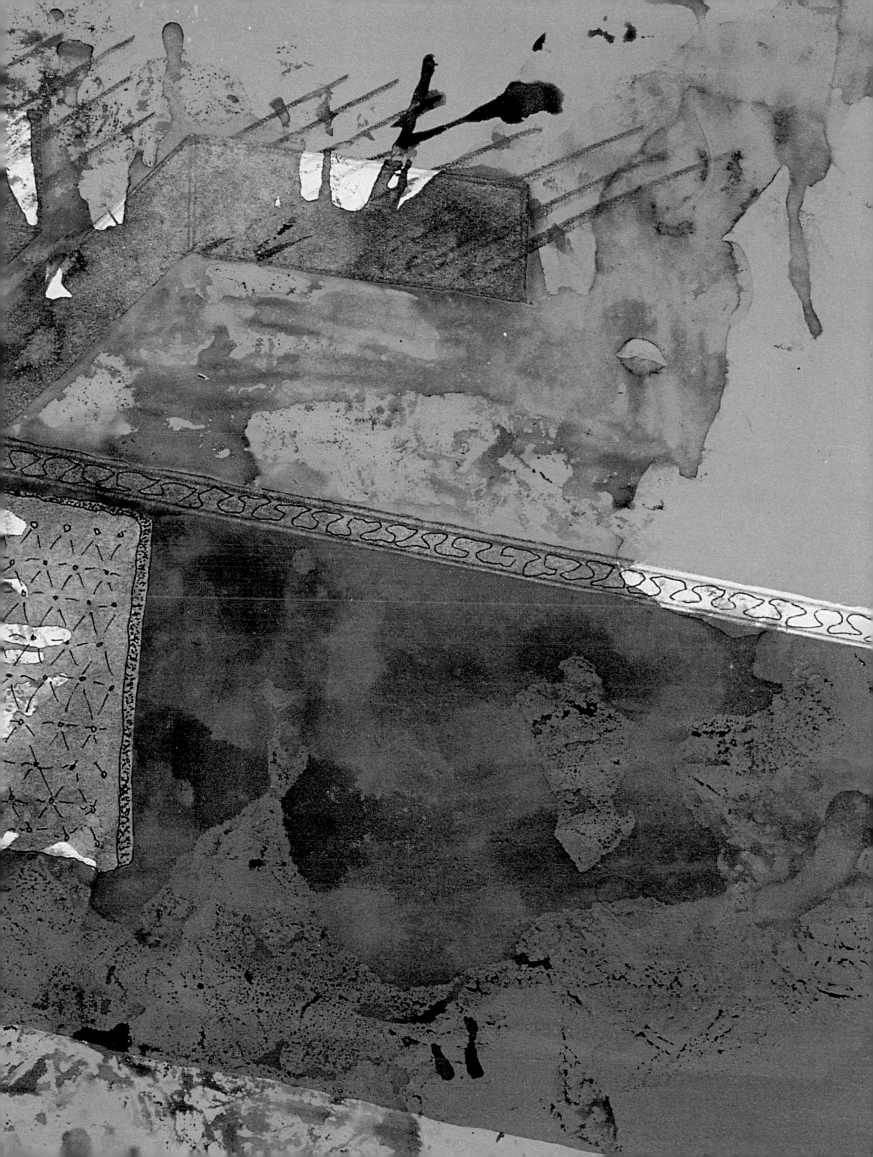

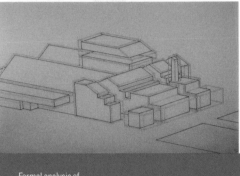

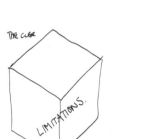

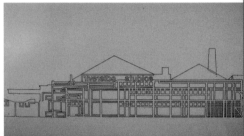

Formal analysis of
Riverside Studios,
Hammersmith,
1979.

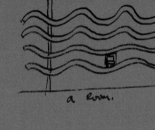

George Finch and
Joan McArthy,
colleagues at
Roderick Ham &
Partners, 1978.

62

During the scorchingly hot summer of 1976, Price's office became a seriously uncomfortable
place to work. Alsop suggested – and Price accepted – an arrangement whereby work would start
at 7.00 a.m. and continue, without a break, until 2.00 p.m., leaving the sultry afternoons free.

It was an attempt to translate the ethos of Rome to London. In those afternoons Alsop taught in David Greene's unit at
the AA. 'It was a period when I was exploring what architecture really meant to me', he says. 'Need it be a personal
artistic expression? Couldn't it be a collective art?'

From the time of his return from Rome, Alsop was also teaching sculpture at Martin's School of Art, an institution
which he sees as a fundamental influence on his career. (He continued teaching there until 1981.) Initially Alsop taught
art history, but he soon became involved in the work of the sculpture department (see p.26). Sculpture at St Martin's
was then dominated by what Alsop calls 'the heavy welders', who were inspired by Anthony Caro and Philip King.
'There was a stress on technique', Alsop recalls. 'The emphasis was on skill – but being able to physically create
something doesn't make you an artist. It's the idea that counts'. Working with Gareth Jones and Roy Ascot, Alsop

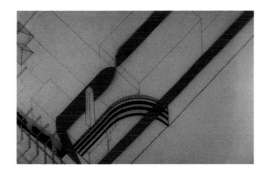

PLAN INTO
PERSPECTIVE

Riverside Studios
project, 1979–81.

Crisp Road
elevation, Riverside
Studios.

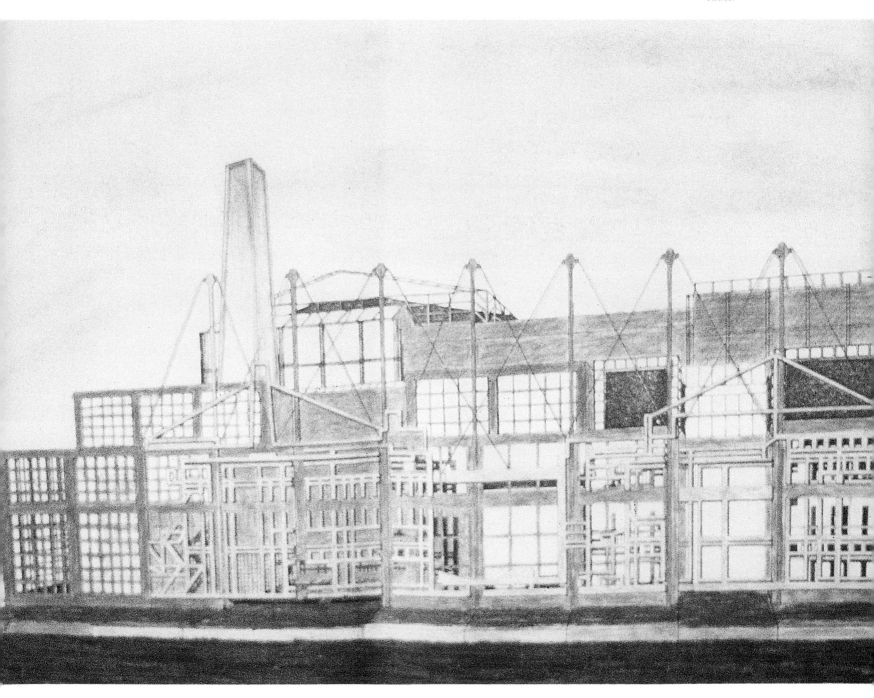

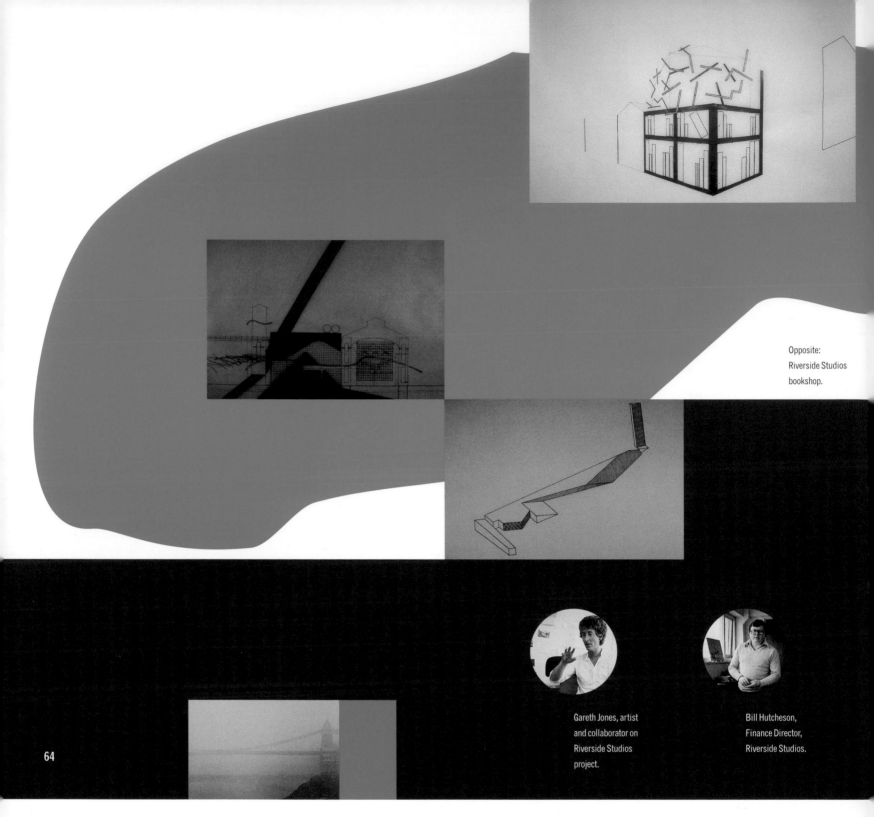

Opposite:
Riverside Studios
bookshop.

Gareth Jones, artist
and collaborator on
Riverside Studios
project.

Bill Hutcheson,
Finance Director,
Riverside Studios.

developed his own sculpture unit, with a very different emphasis. Alsop has always been critical of the 'literary'
nature of architectural practice, its preoccupation with ideas and concern with the intellect over the eye.
Always in sight was the proposition to create a building rather to embark on an open-ended adventure.
'At the art school, there was no propositioned side to the
work and to this end all work was finished and stood or
fell by the response it stimulated'.

ArtNet, of which Alsop became an active member, was the idea of Peter Cook, Cedric Price and
Alastair McAlpine and was an attempt to bring together architects and artists in a stimulating
environment. Amongst the figures whom Alsop met through his membership of the ArtNet circle was
Peter Smithson (who had taught for many years at the AA but whom Alsop had never got to know).
Younger architects in this circle included Mark Fisher and Alsop's near contemporary at the AA, Paul Shepheard.
ArtNet staged a show of 'Five Young Architects', including Alsop, Fisher and Shepheard – 'you felt that you were really

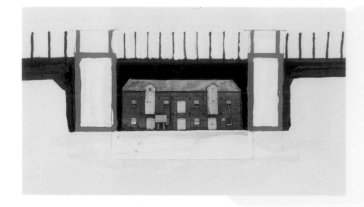

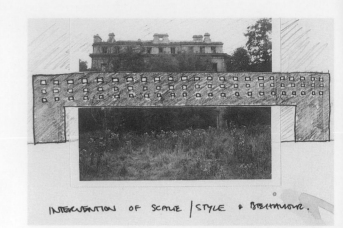

INTERVENTION OF SCALE / STYLE & BEHAVIOUR.

Exercises in
deconstructive
architecture, 1980.

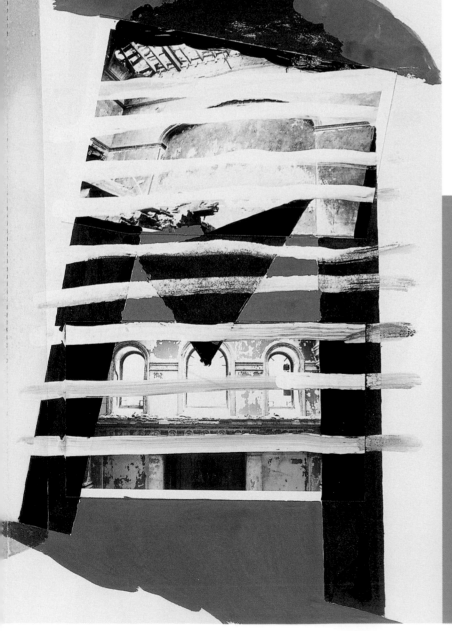

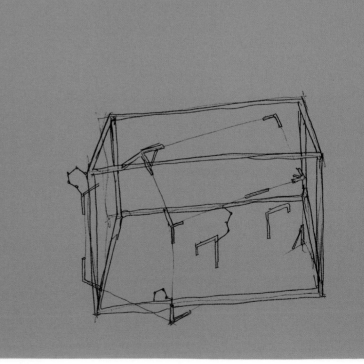

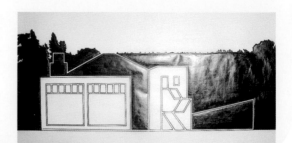

… being able to physically create something doesn't make you an artist

Peter Menby (now
a priest), one of
Alsop's first
employees, 1980.

David Gotthard,
Artistic Director,
Riverside Studios.

a name – an architect in your own right', says Alsop. (McAlpine bought all Alsop's drawings from the show.) It was ironic, in fact, that the AA itself was turning away from the free ambience which had been so much to Alsop's taste. Under its new chairman, Alvin Boyarsky, a more disciplined approach prevailed – for Alsop, the school lost much of its spontaneity and creativity. 'But then I was not one of his protégés!', Alsop admits.

At the heart of ArtNet, for Alsop, was the search for a new definition of architecture (see p.34). There were some notable invited speakers: Colin Rowe, all five of the New York Five, Richard Buckminster Fuller ('I made him a cup of tea', Alsop recalls) and Joseph Beuys. ArtNet lasted three years, a year longer than Price (who believes that organisations should fold whilst they are strong) had advocated.

By the standards of a later generation, Alsop's training had been, while intense and varied, remarkably insular. He had scarcely been abroad. Being invited to take up a visiting teaching post at Ball State University in Indiana

Cromer Pier,
Norfolk.

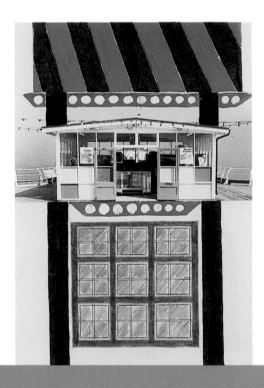

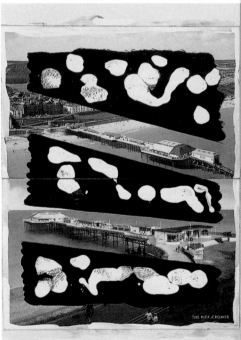

in 1977 was an eye-opener (see pp.55 and 58). Like
Rogers and Foster some years earlier, Alsop was
immediately impressed by the 'can do' approach of the
USA. His introduction to the country was unusual.

After arriving at Indianapolis airport, he was driven, at his own suggestion, blindfolded, to what he describes as 'a log cabin'. There he spent two days, meeting the students, whose project was to help him form a mental picture of the place. When he finally emerged to tour the town, he was bitterly disappointed – it was frankly dull and depressing. Ball State was a very conventional American institution and Alsop recalls incurring the wrath of a caretaker, who took grave exception to his using his office as a studio to paint – such activities were not expected from an architecture tutor.

Nonetheless, the American posting was put to good use. Alsop went to lecture in San Francisco and Philadelphia. He was greatly impressed by the Californian work of Richard Neutra and actually stayed in a house by Neutra, as well as in the Greene brothers' Gamble House in Pasadena. But it was the American landscape, typically, as much as the architecture which impressed him –

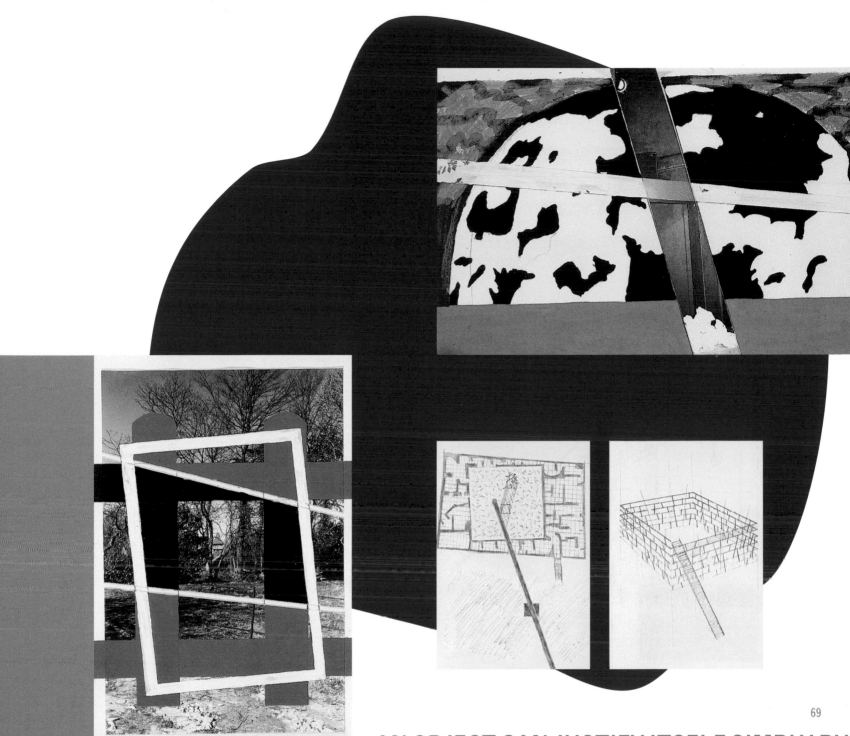

AN OBJECT CAN JUSTIFY ITSELF SIMPLY BY

A good piece of
architecture at
Wells-next-the-Sea,
Norfolk.

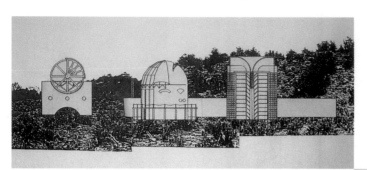

Housing project for
Taos, New Mexico.

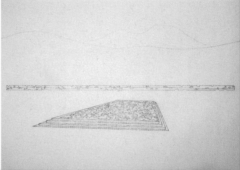

Arts Centre, Taos.

The Queen Mary,
Long Beach,
California.

The barn of
Art Schaller, a
colleague at Ball
State, Indiana.

Indiana barns.

BEING BEAUTIFUL

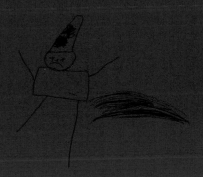

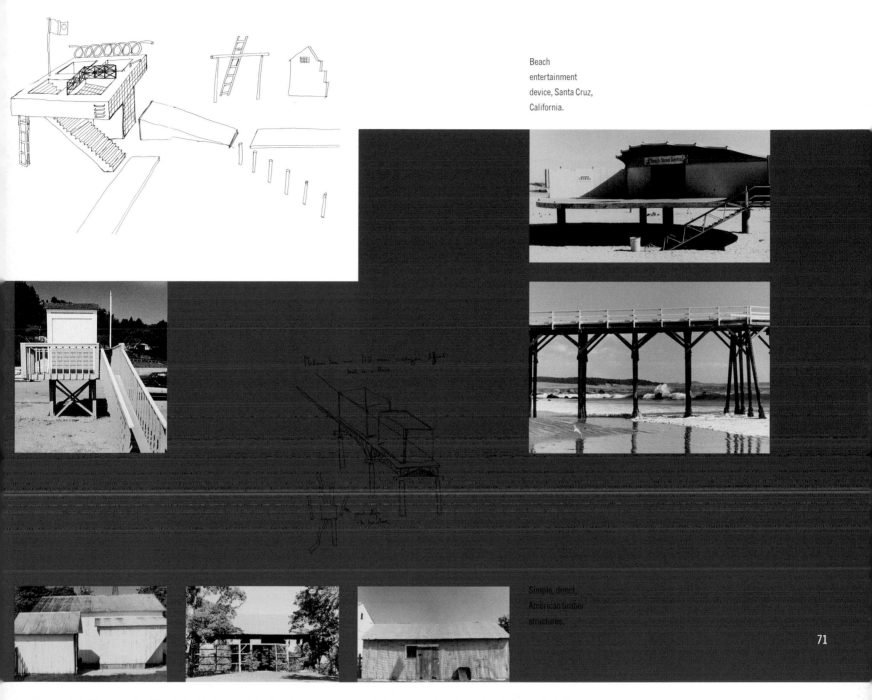

Beach entertainment device, Santa Cruz, California.

Simple, direct, American timber structures.

'vast and varied', Alsop recalls. 'I finally had to learn to drive to get around the country'. He was also, inevitably, struck by New York City, where he caught up with Bernard Tschumi (who was living in one of the first 'lofts') and rushed around art galleries and museums, including Wright's Guggenheim (where, at a private view, most of the guests were distributed along the ramp, rather than in the galleries, 'as if they were gathered to discover where the real art was…' Amongst those to whom Alsop got to speak was Philip Johnson.) Another formative stage in Alsop's architectural education had been accomplished.

While Alsop was in the United States, his first child, Oliver, was born. On his return to Britain, the need to earn a living was again paramount. With Britain still in recessionary mood, and commissions hard to come by, it seems hardly surprising that Alsop, still only 30, did not feel confident enough to found his own practice. Instead, he went to work for Roderick Ham, a well-regarded specialist in theatre work (see p.62).

The two years that Alsop spent with Ham were, he recalls, enjoyable and formative. Ham's office — agreeably informal in its approach — was close to Alsop's home and he could come home for lunch — 'I'd left the 'campus' around Bedford Square and Tottenham Court Road and life seemed very different'.

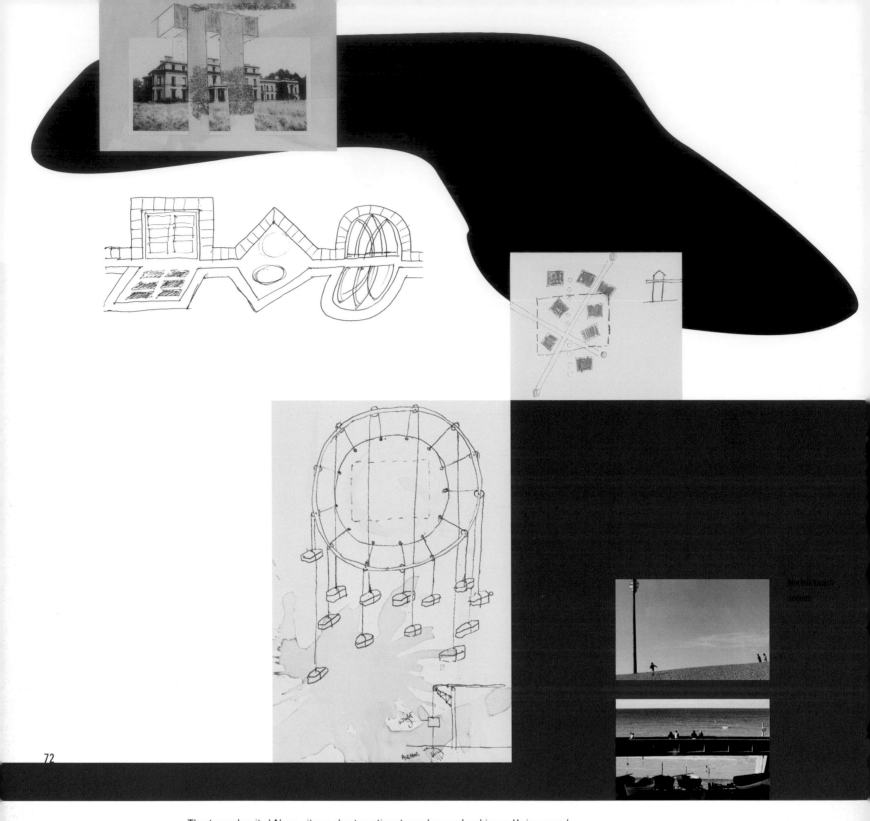

Norfolk beach scenes

Theatre work suited Alsop – it was about creating atmosphere and ambience. He immersed himself readily in the firm's jobs, which included a refurbishment of the Theatre Royal in York as well as a decorative scheme for Chelsea Town Hall. These were projects far removed from Alsop's core interests, but he remembers them as interesting and rewarding.

It was unlikely, of course, that Alsop would confine himself to work of this kind. In his spare time, he worked hard on his own projects, sometimes solo and sometimes with John Lyall. With Cedric Price's old collaborator, Frank Newby, he entered a competition for a river pier planned by the GLC for Westminster. He won the competition but the pier was never built, despite an attempt to revive the project for another client.

It was around this time that Alsop became acquainted with another institution which, like the AA, St Martin's and the Price atelier, was to be an important influence on his career.

In the late Seventies, the stretch of the north bank of the Thames just downstream of Hammersmith Bridge was occupied by a run of utilitarian industrial buildings which formed a barrier between the river and the residential

Westminster Pier
competition winner,
1980.

The painter Bruce
McLean with Alsop
in box of behaviour
at Riverside
Studios, 1980.

Riverside project,
Mark II.

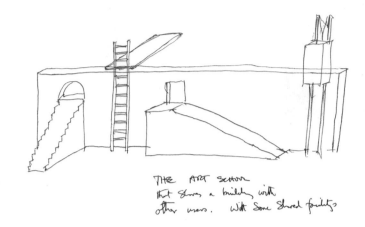

THE ART SCHOOL
that shares a building with
other users. With Some Shared facilities

Riverside bookshop,
1979.

Dick Knox.

The bookshop.

Guests at the
Riverside
Architecture
opening, 1981.

Robin Evans.

Michael Manser and
Sir Hugh Willat.

Bernie Kaye.

John Lyall,
Jane Quinn,
Erica Boulton.

Willy the
roadsweeper and
Gareth Jones.

Joan and John Kent.

Roz and Cliff
Barnett.

streets beyond. Not until 1983 did Richard Rogers and his partners acquire the former oil depot which became their offices (and subsequently part of a 'campus' which now includes the River Café, a series of workspaces and a residential development). Riverside Studios, which opened in 1978 under the auspices of an independent trust, using a pair of former film studios – they had later been used by the BBC for the *Doctor Who* series – was therefore a pioneering venture. The success of the venture led to proposals for the remaining industrial buildings and vacant land on the site to be colonised – the finished complex would house a theatre, cinema, artists' studios, gallery, and cafe.

Alsop's first project for the site (designed in association with Gareth Jones) was basically a conversion of what existed, a modest enough proposal, but an important step forward for a young architect. Alsop believes that the collaboration with Jones was pioneering – 'you didn't hear much about art and architecture in those days', he points out. 'Gareth and I had an understanding: we could just work away together, without talking'.

Alsop recalls having to present his Riverside scheme to such awesomely senior figures as Denys Lasdun and Hugh Casson, who were advising the client – he was relieved to hear his work praised. Beneath the stylistic trappings, there

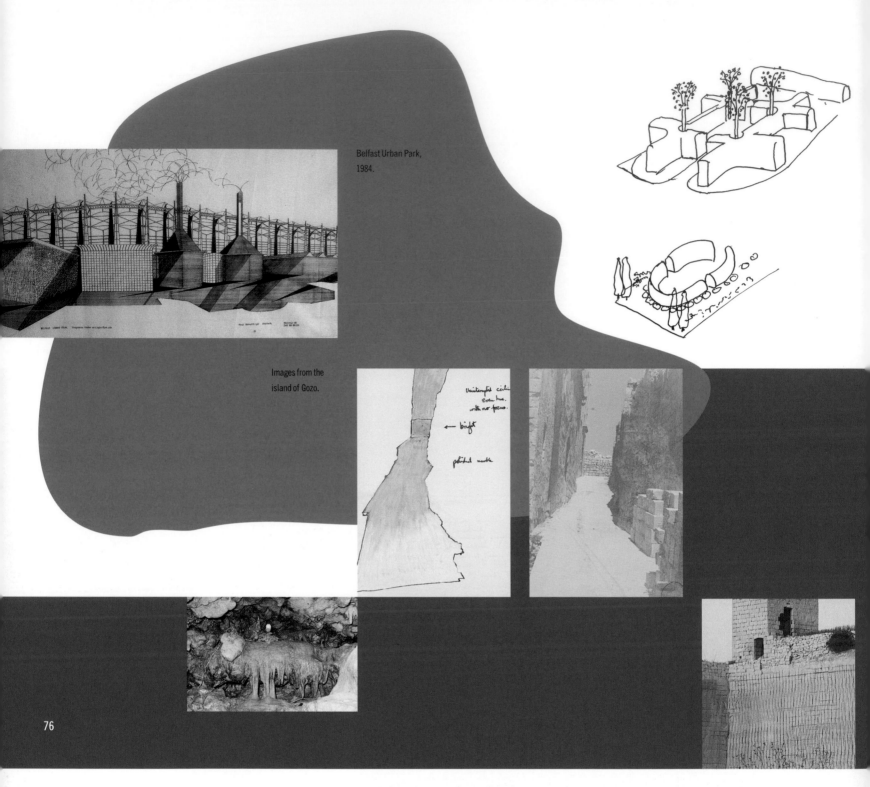

Belfast Urban Park,
1984.

Images from the
island of Gozo.

was, in fact, an imaginative and practical approach to developing the site in an incremental fashion. With the local authority backing the Riverside project and the prospect that it could benefit from the new London property boom (which followed on from the election of the Thatcher government in 1979) by including an element of commercial space, Riverside seemed to have huge potential.

A second, much more ambitious, scheme was developed, incorporating proposals for the development of the rest of the site. This scheme seems, in retrospect, surprisingly Post-Modernist in character. He was, in truth, searching for a style, a way out of the dead-end of late modernism and the even more sterile avenue of vernacular revival, which had enjoyed a brief vogue in the Seventies. On the basis of the Riverside job, Alsop finally set up his own office, working at first from space which he and Lyall had rented from Richard Rogers at Avonmore Road, West Kensington. From there, he moved into a space at Riverside Studios, where he remained until 1984.

In fact, within a couple of years, with the local council having withdrawn its support, Riverside Studios was forced to look at more modest plans — it developed into a popular arts centre for west London, but never the major institution for

Riverside Studios:
adjacent site study.

After the AA and my time with Cedric, Riverside amounted to a third course in architecture

CAnal/CAnal

POOL/BEACH/bug

Fay-do-do
structure, New
Orleans, 1985.

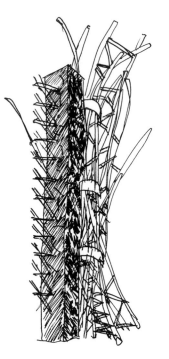

Study for a tall
building, 1983.

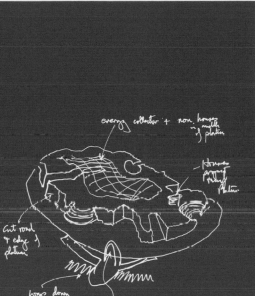

you didn't hear much about art and architecture in those days

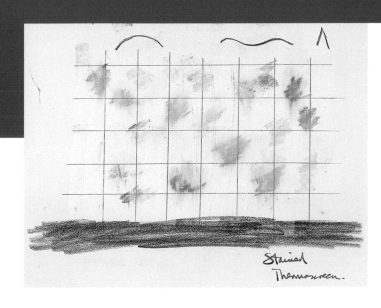

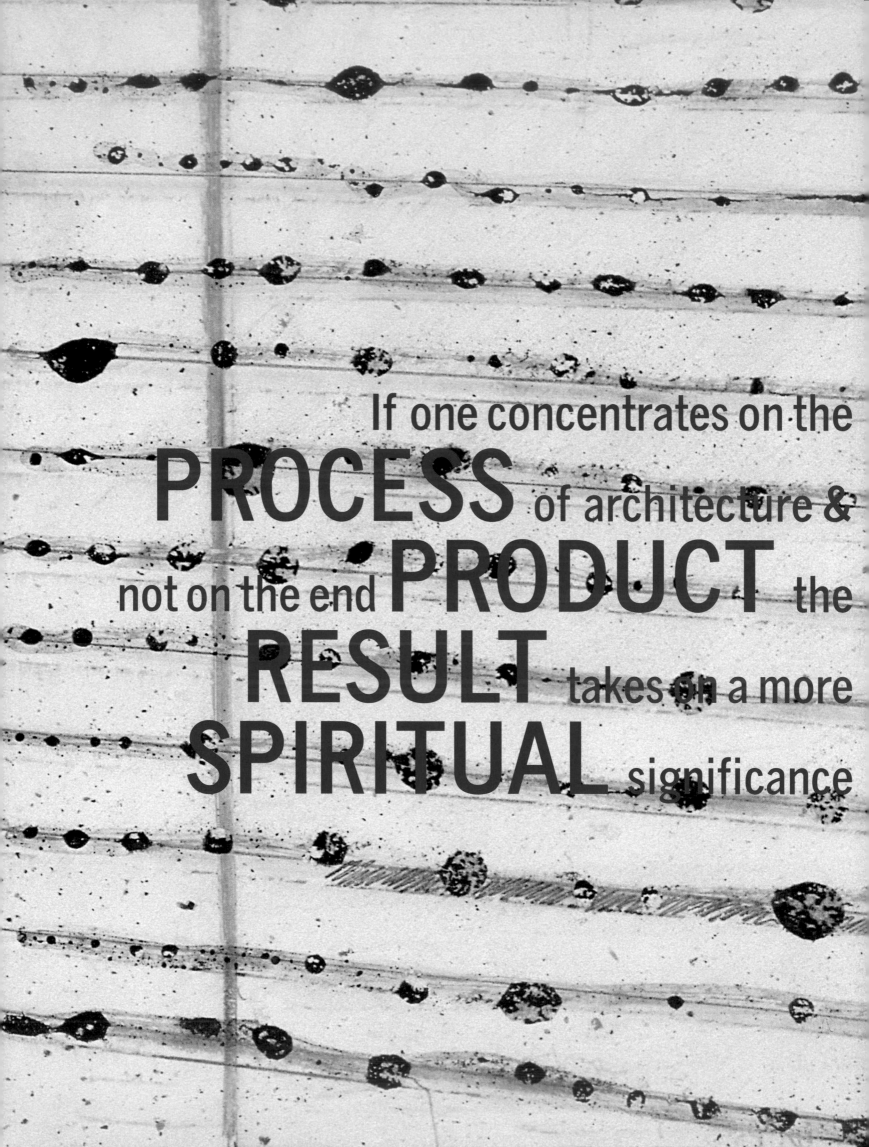

If one concentrates on the **PROCESS** of architecture & not on the end **PRODUCT** the **RESULT** takes on a more **SPIRITUAL** significance

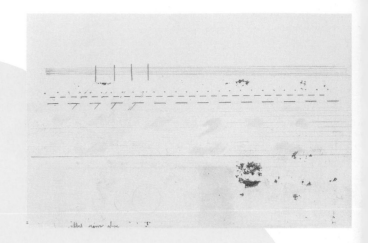

Casino for Orlando,
Florida, 1985.

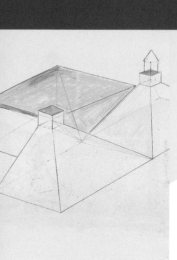

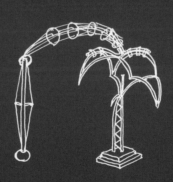

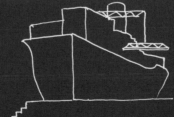

Opposite:
Orlando Casino.

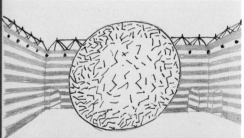

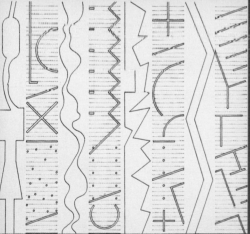

Alternative art
school plan.

Amanda Marshel,
office collaborator.

Study for a house
extension and
alteration.

Plan for a new art
school, Gwent,
Wales, 1982.

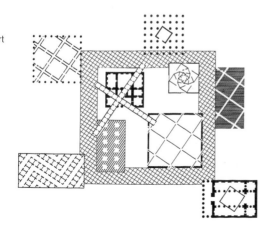

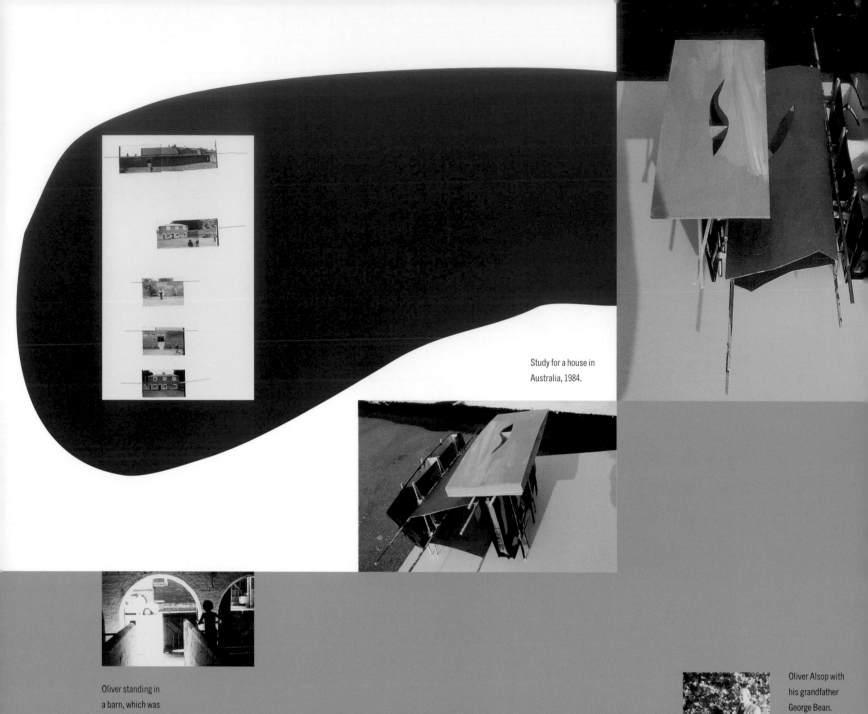

Study for a house in
Australia, 1984.

Oliver standing in
a barn, which was
later converted into
a house.

Oliver Alsop with
his grandfather
George Bean.

a time envisaged. Nonetheless, Riverside left its mark on Alsop. (Its bookshop was actually his first built scheme; see p.75.) He remembers sometime director Peter Gill as a huge talent. Under Gill's leadership, Riverside attracted some notable talents. Alsop recalls the bar there as a remarkable meeting place.

Amongst those he got to know were Samuel Beckett (visiting to direct one of his own plays) and Van Morrison. It was at Riverside that Alsop first met artist Bruce McLean, with whom he was to form an ongoing collaboration. 'After the AA and my time with Cedric, Riverside amounted to a third course in architecture', says Alsop. But by the time that Alsop & Lyall moved out of Riverside, the air of optimism there had rather evaporated: 'frankly, it had become a bit depressing and I was glad to get out', says Alsop.

In January, 1981 the informal partnership with John Lyall which had grown out of MultiMatch and continued on an *ad hoc* basis was given formal status with the launch of Alsop & Lyall. John Lyall (b.1949) had an interestingly varied c.v. He had worked for Cedric Price for a short period and for Piano & Rogers at the time of the Pompidou project, as well

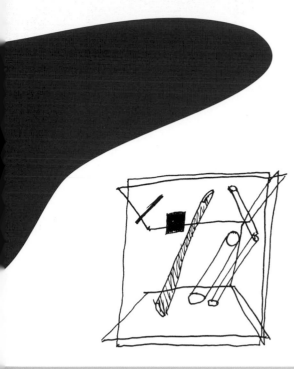

Model fo Cairo
Conference Centre,
1982.

A PLACE WITHOUT RULES

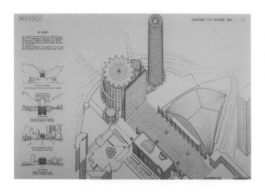 

Entry for the
Defense
Competition, Paris.

An opening house.

Overleaf:
The Great Screen
for the Defense
competition, Paris.

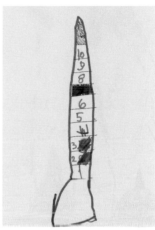

89

The duck pond,
Holland Park,
London.

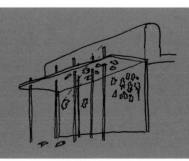

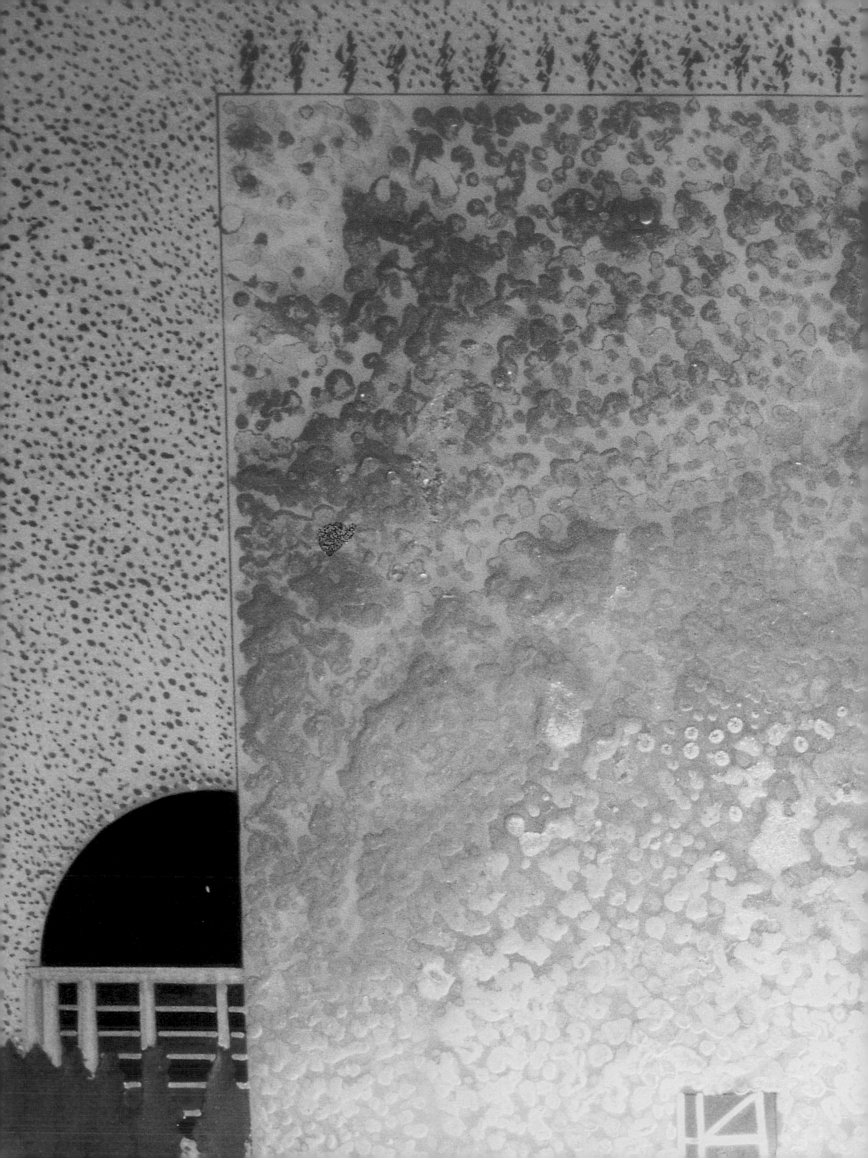

Opposite:
Study for the
Hafenstrasse
housing project on
the banks of the
Elbe, Hamburg.

each project determines its own rules and sensibilities

New haystack
technology changes
the rural aesthetic.

92

as for a series of more obviously 'commercial' practices. Lyall's architectural taste inclined, more than Alsop's,

towards the High-tech, though he was also to develop a strong interest in conservation and rehabilitation. (Alsop has

always seen himself as 'a consumer of technology, not an innovator'.)

The two architects were to spend nearly a decade in partnership. Architectural partnerships, like marriages, often

end painfully and the break-up of Alsop & Lyall was not easy. Nonetheless, the partnership can be seen as a creative

period for Alsop. 'The office specialises in architecture in the broadest possible way', one of its early brochures stated.

'We enjoy what we do'. Maintaining an open mind, in order to avoid a formulaic approach, was a basic tenet –

'each project determines its own rules and sensibilities which have to be recognised and understood.

These indeterminate factors mould the architecture'.

The collapse of the Riverside project, however, did not

augur well for the success of Alsop & Lyall. The practice

actively pursued work. It entered the 1982 competition

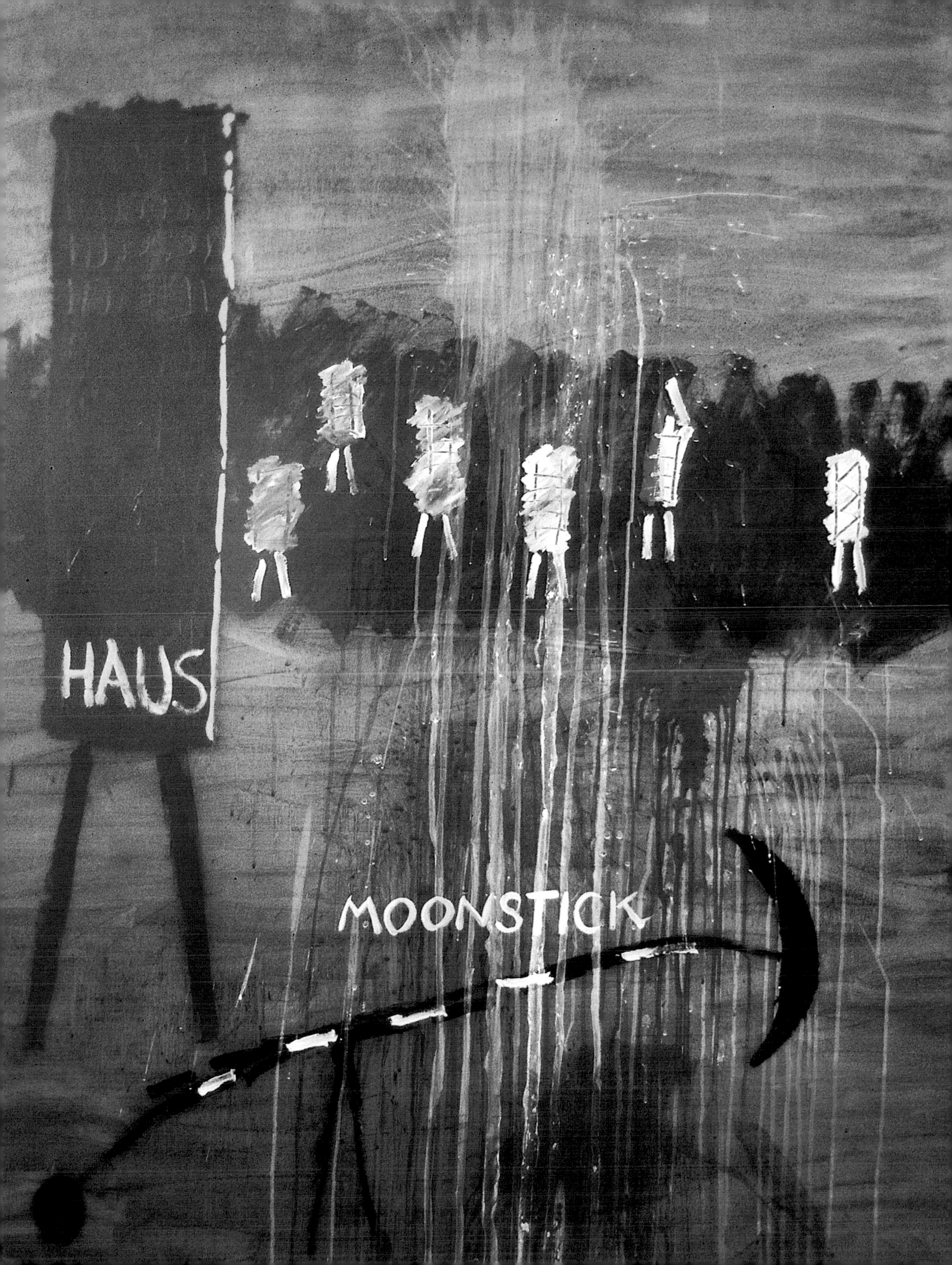
HAUS
MOONSTICK

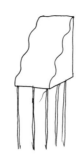

Study for temporary
theatre structure for
Groningen, The
Netherlands.

Bauforum,
Hamburg, 1985.

95

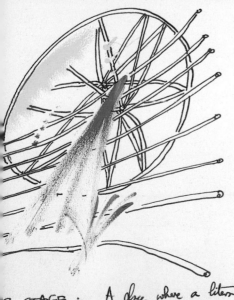

Bauforum project
(1985) on the site of
the Alsop ferry
terminal.

STAGE :- A place where a literal new
perspective can be found.

Material Solidity on 'stage' is not important

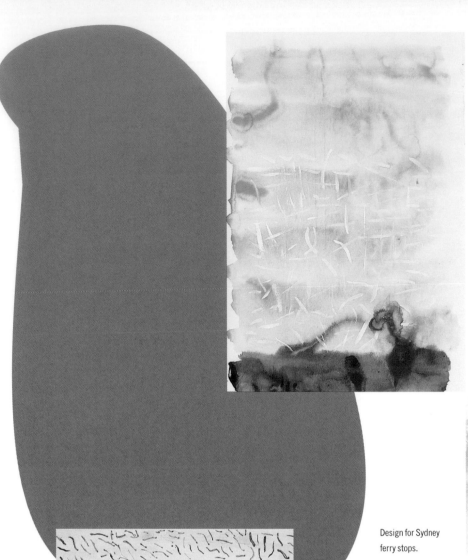

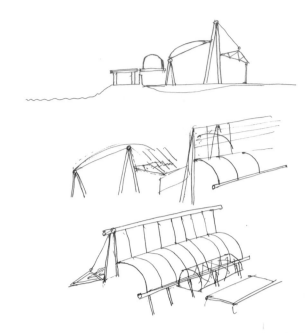

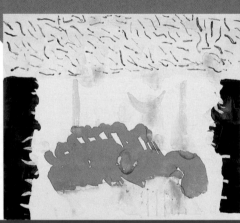

Design for Sydney
ferry stops.

Ball House, Sydney,
by Glen Murcutt.

Architect Brit
Andresen in
Queensland.

Alsop on the farm in
Victoria.

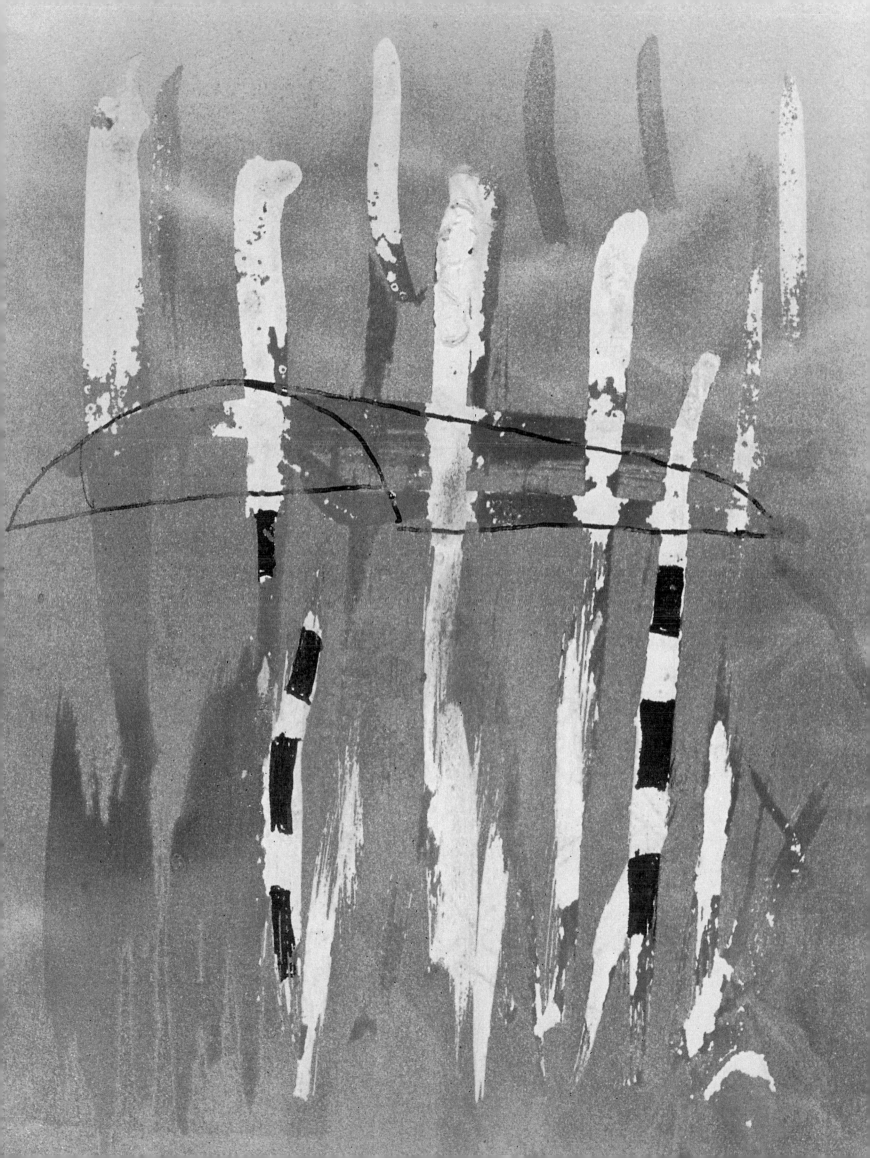

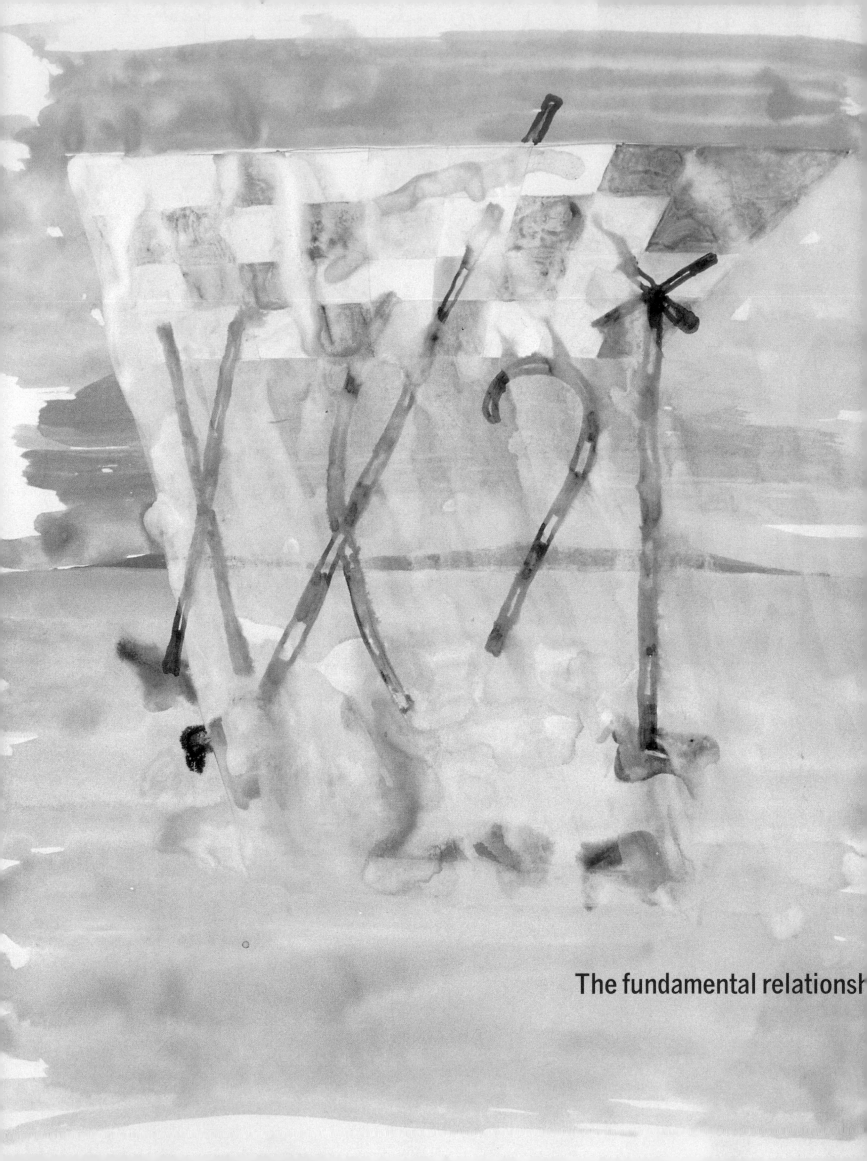

The fundamental relationsh

Workshop group
at the Royal
Melbourne Institute
of Technology,
1984.

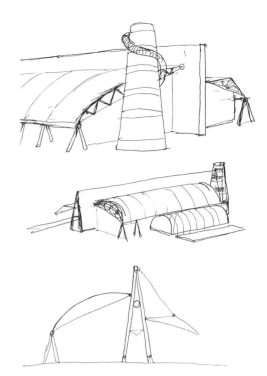

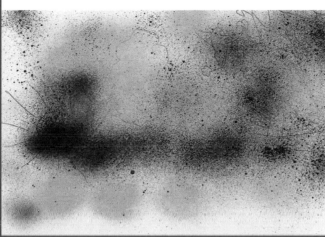

Margot Hutcheson
growing bilberries
in Queensland.

Geoff Warne on the
Indian Ocean,
Perth.

Peg Quarry at Eden.

99

Opposite:
Sydney roof.

for a new landmark building at La Defense in Paris,
proposing a massive screen, 'a façade that is, by its
nature, a true reflection of the building's function as
well as a unique late-twentieth-century monument'.

The screen would address a great new public square. Behind would be a circular block containing an exhibition and information centre, featuring a moving floor
(an echo of Piano & Rogers' idea for the Pompidou Centre), attached to a tall circular tower using an innovative glazing system intended to give the building an
ethereal look – it was an odd premonition of the later Tour sans Fin, designed by Alsop's friend Jean Nouvel. The punctilious detailing proposed in Alsop &
Lyall's (unsuccessful) submission probably reflected Lyall's High-tech background, but the core of the proposal was its strong urban form.

CLIENT ARCHITECT

'The whole family of buildings are seen as a family of pure elemental forms that, although separated, have a maternal
homogeneity as they are clustered behind the great screen on a pure horizontal 'table' or plinth'. Another competition
scheme was that for the extension to London's National Gallery, which attracted some of the leading practitioners,
including Stirling and Rogers, and was eventually won by Ahrends, Burton & Koralek. (After their scheme was
dropped, following an intervention by the Prince of Wales, the job went to the American Robert Venturi.)

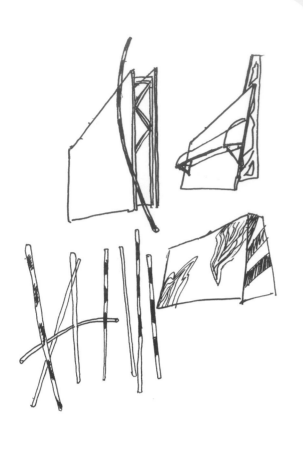

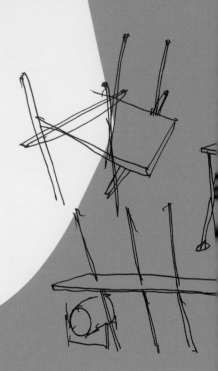

The Eagle pub
conversion in
Farringdon,
London, 1985.

Alsop with his
son Piers.

100

Alsop & Lyall's entry, which boldly separated out the requisite enabling commercial development, was largely the work
of Alsop and represented a bold move towards full blooded Post-Modernism of a sort he was soon to reject. There
were also competition schemes for a conference centre in Egypt (a tensile structure) and for a resort in New Mexico.
The last was seen as a very serious proposition and could have been a breakthrough for the office. The 325-hectare
(800-acre) site was in the wilderness – 'there seemed to be every kind of wildlife, including rattlesnakes', says Alsop.
'Part of it was occupied by an abandoned hippy colony, complete with rotting geodesic domes' (see p.70). On a visit
there, Alsop stayed in a hotel where D.H. Lawrence had lived in the 1920s – the owner could remember the Englishman
and possessed an amazing collection of Lawrence's paintings. The project was, however, over-ambitious and it came
to nothing. The firm did win the competition for new housing at Rainbow Quays in London's Docklands, but, to their
chagrin, the scheme, in a brick Post-Modern manner, remained unbuilt (see p.136–7).

Within three years, Alsop & Lyall, though attracting a lot of critical interest, was 'desperate' for
work. It was fortunate to attract interest from the Department of Environment in Northern Ireland,

Thought on a table
for the Eagle pub
conversion.

Proposal for a
cultural theme park
in collaboration
with Peter Gabriel
and Realworld Ltd,
at Darling Harbour,
Sydney, 1986.

Isobel Lousada and
Jonathan Adams,
members of the
Alsop office, on
board en route to
Hamburg.

Sheila, Oliver and
Nancy saying
goodbye to Alsop at
Sheringham
Station, Norfolk.

Model for an extension to the Kunsthalle, Hamburg, 1985. The emphasis lay in trying to make the interior give its contents to the streets.

Painting for the
Kunsthalle project
(the first painting
collaboration with
Bruce McLean).

105

Drawings by Alsop
for the Kunsthalle,
Hamburg.

Bremen Hafen
workshop: acres of
welded steel under
a steel sky, 1988.

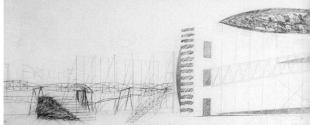

The Shipfish mixed-use complex, Hamburg (1985): a large building with a small address on a street at the top of hill.

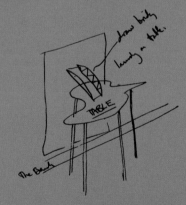

Malcolm Bruno, a composer and friend. Says Alsop: 'One of the most optimistic people I know.'

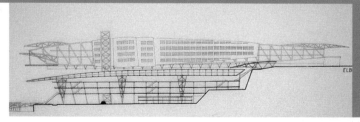

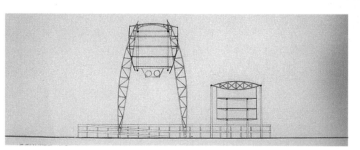

Infrastructural art museum (with Bruce McLean) – a Tate Modern alternative.

Shipfish development, Hamburg.

Overleaf: Innenstadt Ost, a two-street intervention to help regenerate the old commercial heart of the city of Hamburg.

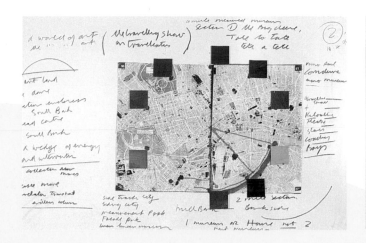

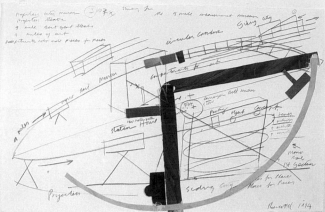

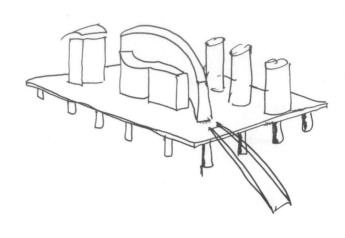

Covered streets,
places for
performance,
platforms of retreat:
the language of
change.

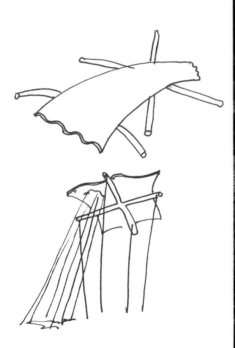

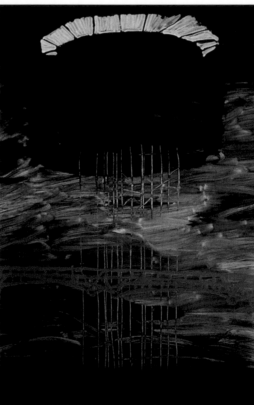

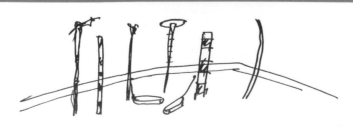

Oliver Alsop in a
Norfolk cornfield.

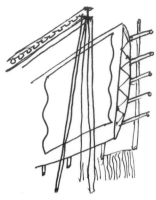

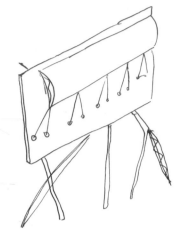

Design for a
temporary theatre,
Groningen.

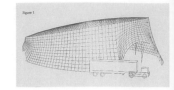

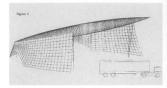

Lego house — part
of a series of
projects related to
parallel worlds.

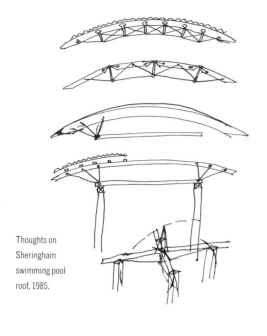

Thoughts on
Sheringham
swimming pool
roof, 1985.

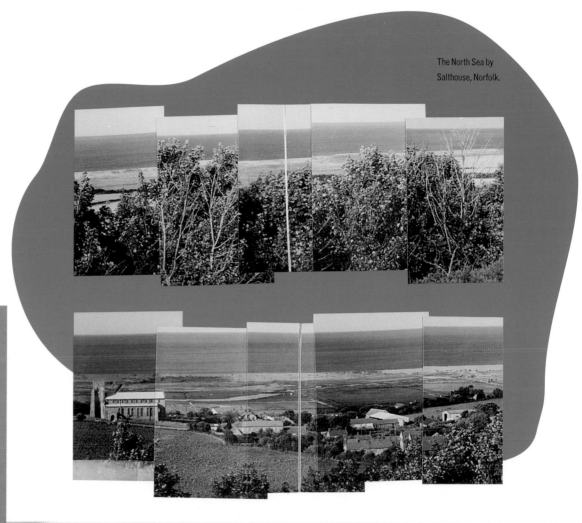

The North Sea by
Salthouse, Norfolk.

Leisure centre in
the garden.

where the De Lorean car factory (which had received big government subsidies) had closed down with a major loss of jobs. The Belfast Urban Park project (1983–4) aimed to reuse the factory site – located on the critical divide between Republican and Loyalist areas of the city – for a regenerative development vaguely rooted in 'leisure'.

According to Alsop, 'Belfast seemed to have plenty of leisure facilities – the point was that people needed jobs'. Alsop's focus was on education and training as much as entertainment. He wanted to work with the local community to create what was, in effect, a community college on a grand scale, a harbinger of later projects (perhaps most obviously, C-Plex). This would be a highly flexible space, hung along a central spine, with a retractable roof, where basket-weaving and cake-baking, as well as computer training and car repair workshops, could find a niche.

The space would respond to the demands of the 'market' – really the local community and businesses. There would also be an ice-skating rink and an art gallery. There was an echo here, of course, of Price's Interaction, though Alsop envisaged the development as being hugely, inspirationally enjoyable as well as functional – 'Cedric would never countenance talk about the

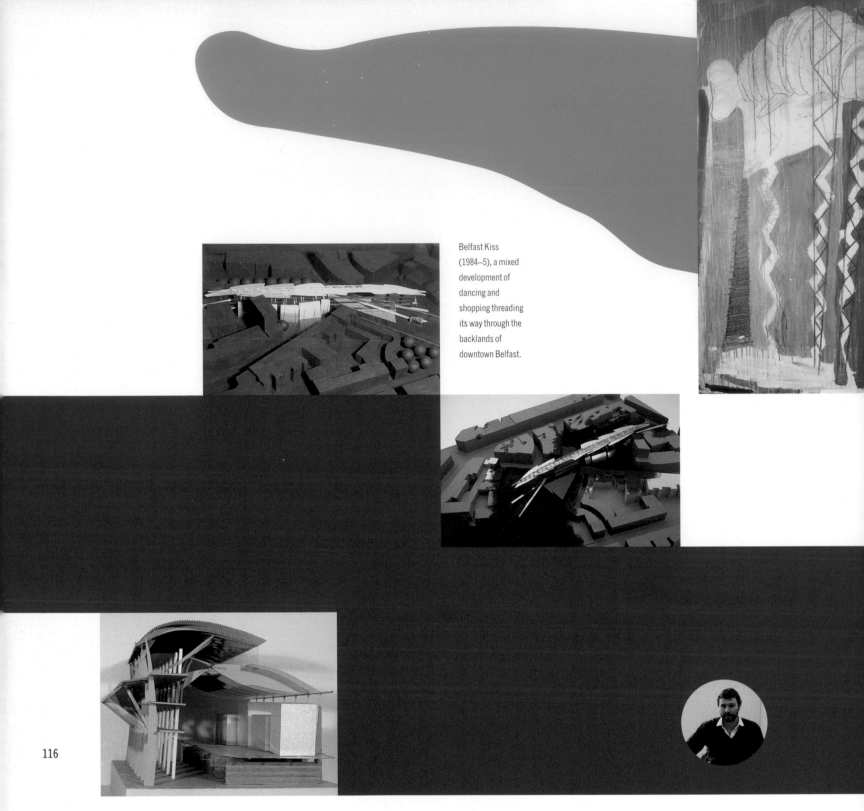

Belfast Kiss (1984–5), a mixed development of dancing and shopping threading its way through the backlands of downtown Belfast.

116

pleasures you get from a space', he says. Working with the local community and responding to the unpredictable views of 'ordinary' people seemed to Alsop to be a proper part of the art of architecture. 'My work is not about designing buildings as free-standing objects', he says. 'To some extent, it's not about designing buildings at all, in the sense of setting out with a clear agenda. The agenda has to emerge as part of the process of design. I compare it to the work of a sculptor, say. No true artist can entirely predict what a completed work will look like – if he can, that work is likely to be a failure'.

The practice had thrown an enormous amount of energy into the Belfast project and it was galling to see it shelved by the government. Alsop's spirits were revived somewhat by his first visit to Australia, a country to which he immediately warmed and was to revisit on many occasions (see pp.86 and 96–9). 'It was invigorating', he says. 'The Australians were not an 'aesthetic' race in the normal sense of the word, but it was a country where architects were encouraged to get on with things, rather than just talk about them'. Alsop remembers the mid-Eighties as 'a betwixt/between period' – he had firmly abandoned the Post-Modernism with which he had briefly toyed but was still looking for a new way. The influence of Cedric Price was still pervasive, but Alsop wanted to develop an approach to design of his own.

The Evans and the
Alsops en route to
another picnic.

Normal Life Takes
Over the Central
Reservation in
Kansas City: study
for an uban project,
1986.

Butler's Wharf bar
and jazz club,
London.

NO SUCH THING AS A MISTAKE IN ARCHITECTURE

Bremen Bahnhof
Platz.

The desert: a relief
from architecture.

Pyramid visitor
centre, Egypt.

Rolling studios.

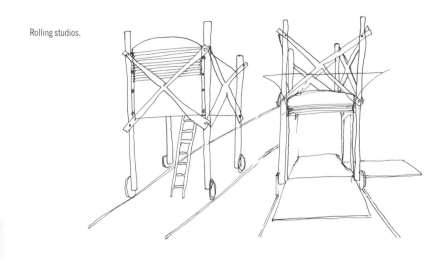

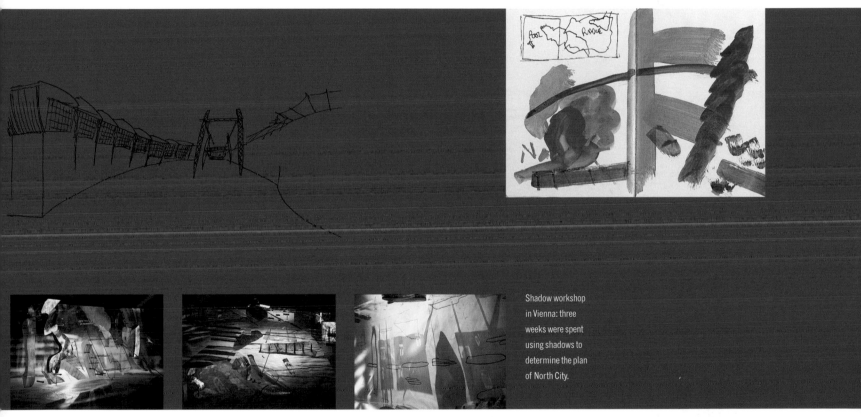

Shadow workshop in Vienna: three weeks were spent using shadows to determine the plan of North City.

To no small degree, the way out of this impasse lay abroad. In fact, this was a good time for British architects to look overseas. With his notorious Hampton Court speech in the summer of 1984, the Prince of Wales had effectively declared war on modern architecture, which was, as he saw it, an inhuman machine wrecking people's lives.

The Prince, having succeeded in the National Gallery saga, went on to rubbish other schemes – developers ran scared and tended to opt for architecture which they thought would appeal to the Prince.

Alsop had always been interested in the innovative art scene in Germany, so that he welcomed the chance to work there. Germany was subsequently to feature strongly in Alsop's career, particularly after he formed a partnership with the Hamburg-based architect Jan Störmer. It was Hamburg, one of Germany's largest cities and a great port, which produced the first German project, a winning entry to the competition for the Innenstadt Ost area of the city, east of the Rathaus (see p.105–6). The invitation to submit came about because Hamburg's chief planner Egbert Kossak had seen coverage of the Riverside scheme in the *Architectural Review* and was interested in a practice which had shown

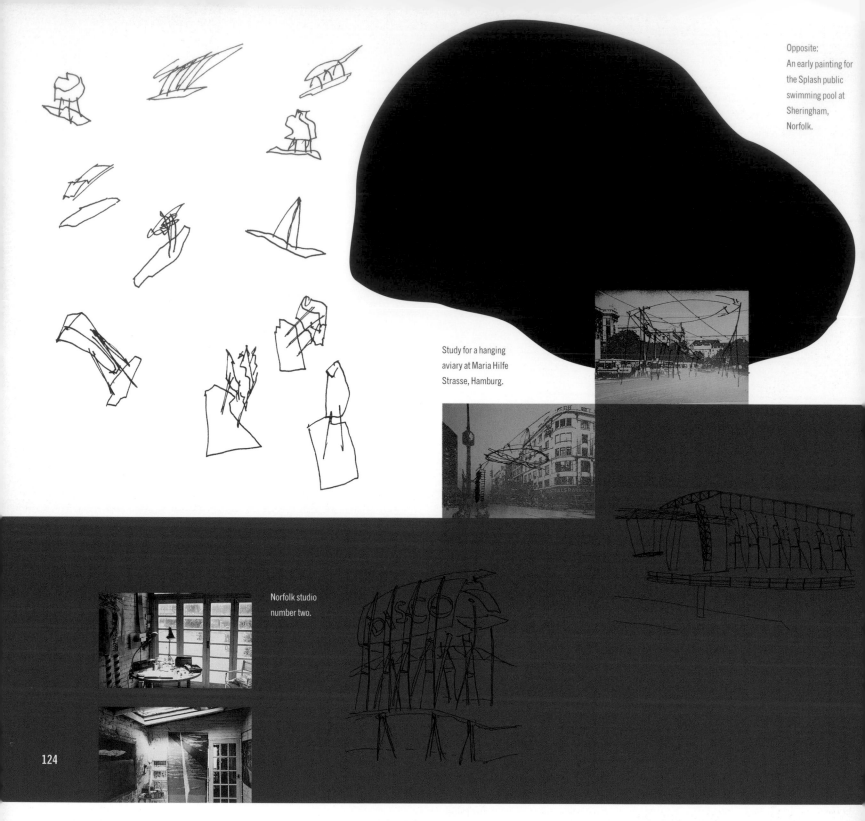

Opposite:
An early painting for
the Splash public
swimming pool at
Sheringham,
Norfolk.

Study for a hanging
aviary at Maria Hilfe
Strasse, Hamburg.

Norfolk studio
number two.

124

promise with a major waterside scheme. Alsop warmed to the city – 'you felt that you could really get something done there', he says. Between 1985 and 1986 Alsop worked on two important projects in this area of Hamburg, where regeneration of obsolete quayside areas was the aim (see pp.92–5).

Shipfish, designed with the help of Tania Riccius and engineer Peter Rice as a competition entry, was a complex of offices and workshops/studios which reached dramatically across a major highway to overhang the river Elbe with its redundant quays. The scheme was dramatically presented, using models and Alsop's own paintings (it was at this stage that painting began to figure prominently in his presentations), but nothing was built (see pp.106–7).

The scheme to extend Hamburg's Kunsthalle produced an ambitious and radical proposal – a genuinely fresh view of the nature of an art museum – including a great covered atrium criss-crossed by bridges which looked forward to the majestic internal space of the Hôtel du Département in Marseilles. Alsop wanted to counter the idea of the art gallery as a progression of spaces – a 'corridor' (see p.104–5).

Visiting Hamburg, Alsop was recruited to participate in the Bauforums which the city had established as a way of involving the citizenry in the process of planning and development –

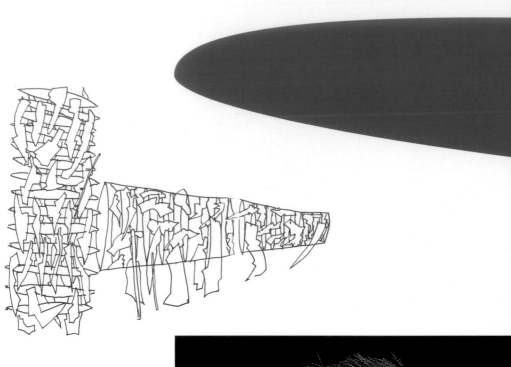

... conversation determined the aesthetic of the room

Schreiber Garden in downtown Bremen. Many locals cycle to their allotments for the weekend.

Personless building.

Car transporter.

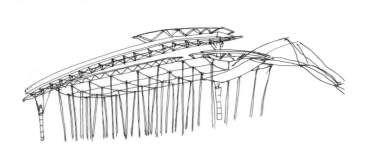

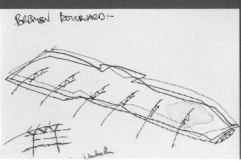

BREMEN BOULEVARD!-

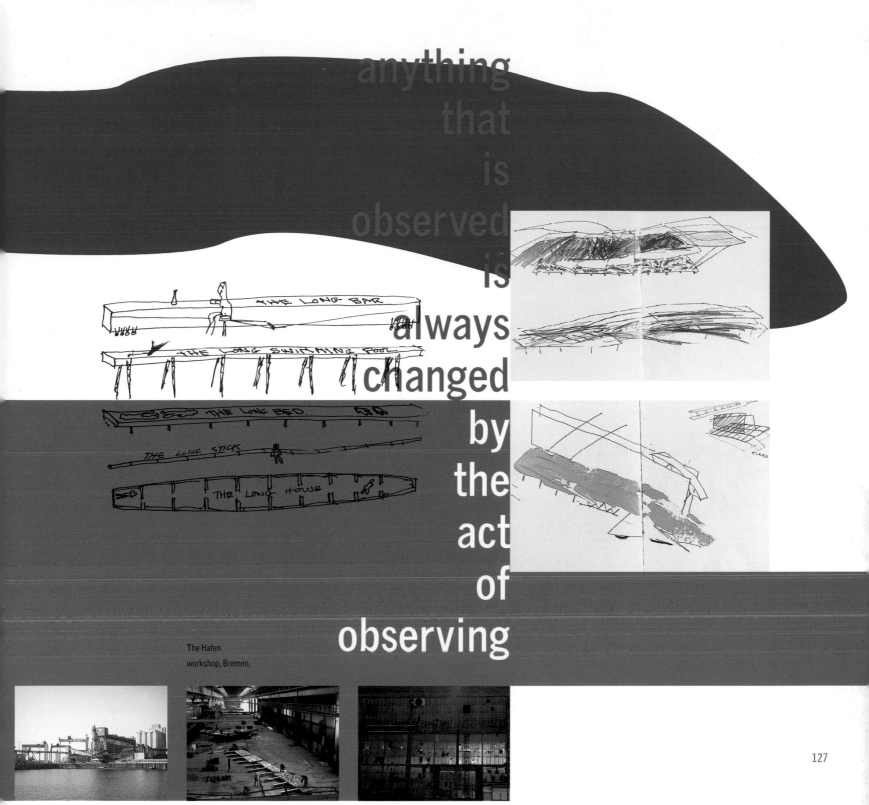

anything that is observed is always changed by the act of observing

THE LONG BAR

THE LONG SWIMMING POOL

THE LONG BED.

THE LONG STICK

THE LONG HOUSE

The Hafen
workshop, Bremen.

sitting in on its meetings strengthened his conviction that community involvement could be a positive force in architecture. 'It was sociable, instructive and even well-paid', says Alsop. 'I have always wondered why London didn't do something similar'. Alsop had also begun to teach in Germany, initially at the Bremen Academy for Art and Music. Alsop has a habit of rapidly colonising any space where he touches down and his office in Bremen soon became another studio – 'conversation determined the aesthetic of the room', he says. Alsop's Bremen workshops became remarkably lively (and taxing) occasions, often extending long into the night.

The Hamburg Ferry Terminal (built 1989–93) was the first major built project generated by Alsop's work in Germany. It emerged out of his involvement with the Bauforum and consultative work with the city planners and also from the earlier Hafenstrasse housing project (unbuilt) in which Bruce McLean had been a collaborator.

The completed terminal was planned as a big building – 500 metres (1,640 feet) long and incorporating a variety of uses: passenger lounges, offices, customs facilities, freight handling space and areas for cars to be checked in prior to loading. Although something of the sculptural

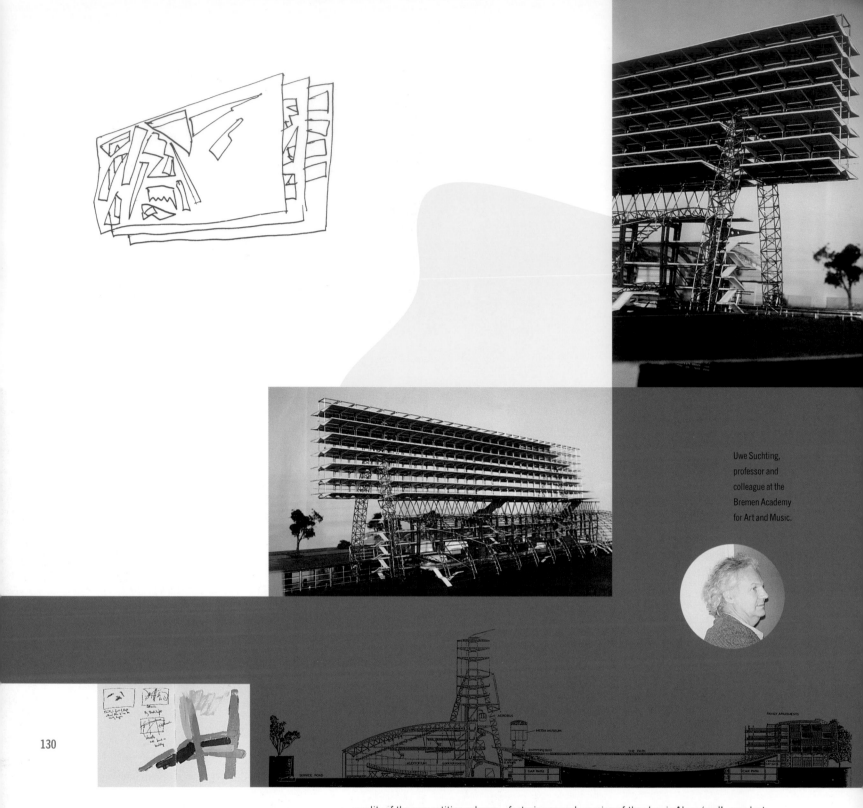

Uwe Suchting, professor and colleague at the Bremen Academy for Art and Music.

quality of the competition scheme – featuring an early version of the classic Alsop 'pod' –was lost in what was built – Alsop was pressured to pack in more space – the terminal is a forceful addition to the Hamburg waterfront, elevated to avoid the seasonal flooding which affects the site.

Built of pre-cast concrete, its aesthetic is frankly industrial/maritime – seen across the water, it appears to be floating, like a great ship. Alsop had certainly come to terms with engineering, but there is also a strong expressive purpose behind the project which extends beyond the functional (see pp.146–53).

Something of the 'infinite' and repetitive character of the Hamburg Terminal can be seen in the unbuilt project for a media centre in Cologne.

Alsop's first meeting with Jean Nouvel, an architect whose work he greatly admires, took place in Paris in 1987. Also in Paris for an architecture biennale was Massimiliano Fuksas from Rome. Soon after, Alsop, Nouvel and Fuksas, plus the Munich-based Otto Steidle, came together to work on one of the more remarkable unbuilt projects of recent years. Hérouville Saint-Clair is a small,

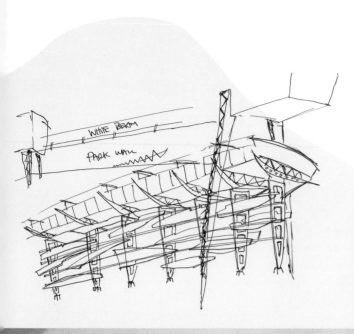

Cologne Media
Park, 1987. Work/
rest/eat/play and,
at the bottom right,
a tomato farm.

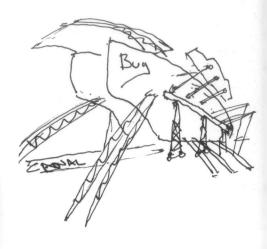

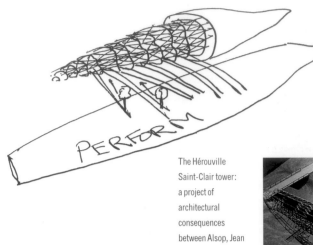

The Hérouville Saint-Clair tower: a project of architectural consequences between Alsop, Jean Nouvel, Otto Steidle and Massimiliano Fuksas.

At the bottom of the tower Alsop produces a bridge of small shops and birds.

Overleaf:
An early sketch for
Hérouville Tower.

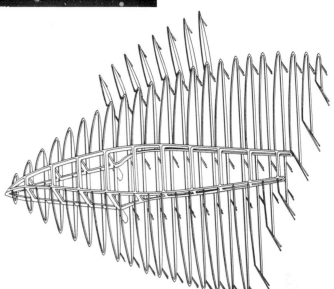

Hendon Aircraft
Museum, London.

A Balmain bug,
Sydney.

This building has arrived as an alien

133

The project evolved
into Centre
Commercial.

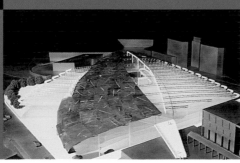

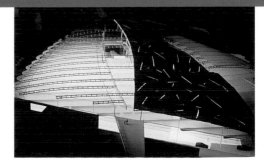

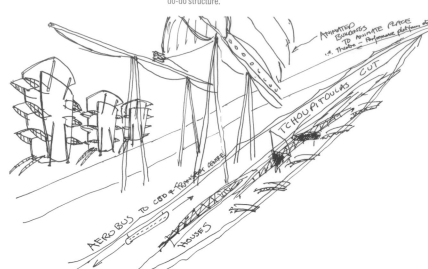

New Orleans fay-
do-do structure.

Rainbow Quays
housing project for
London Docklands.

Sheila, Oliver,
Nancy and Piers
in Paris.

Pisa.

136

unremarkable dormitory town, mostly of post-war date, near Caen in Normandy — not far, in fact,
from the site of what became EuroDisney. The objective behind the the Hérouville Tower project
was, quite simply, to put Hérouville on the map. The idea of the tower came from Hérouville's
mayor, François Geindre, who wanted to give the town a real heart instead of the existing vacuum
of roads and car parks. In historic French cities, high buildings are restricted to the periphery —
hence La Defense. Hérouville was to have a tower at its very core — and what a tower.
Alsop & Lyall's contribution consisted of 'the bits on the ground', a sprawling, zoomorphic structure at the base of the tower, very much in the spirit of the
Hamburg Shipfish project, containing shops and an aviary. Above were piled offices by Fuksas, housing by Steidle and a hotel by Nouvel.

The Hérouville tower was never built. Alsop subsequently developed his part of the project as a
striking, wing-like shopping centre, but this too remained unbuilt. 'I have developed a building
that will act as a bridge to connect the two existing main parts of the town centre', Alsop wrote of
this version of the scheme. 'My proposal creates a specific route along the main east/west axis.

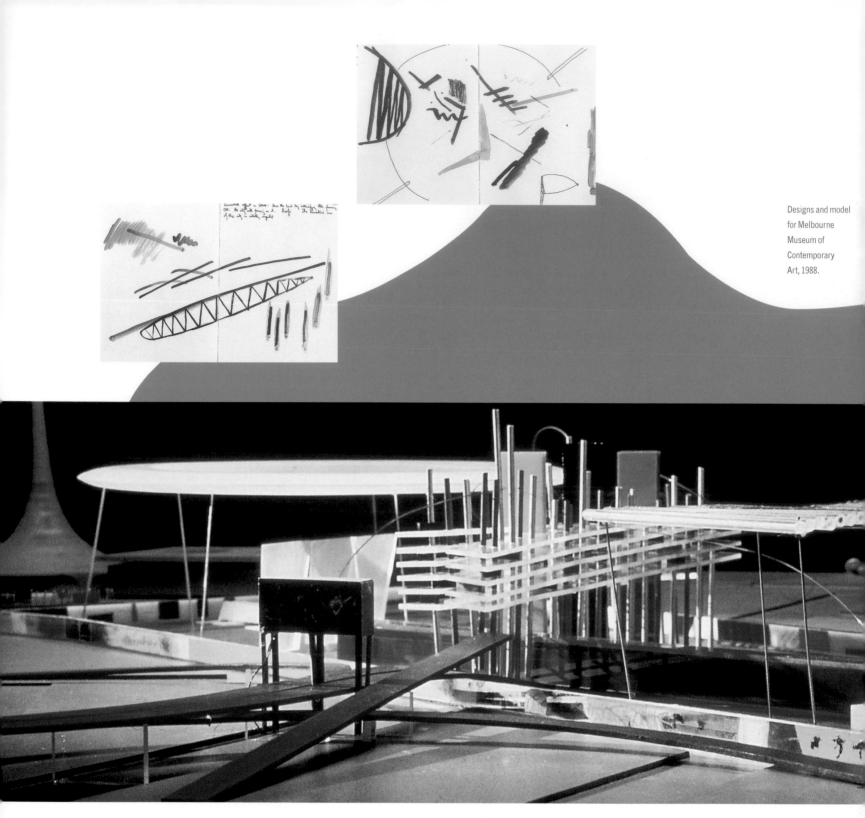

Designs and model
for Melbourne
Museum of
Contemporary
Art, 1988.

It will be possible for the public to begin to experience the centre of the town as a composition of
covered and open spaces, each of which will be addressed by places to eat and rest. In this way,
the intention is to make the centre of the town a combined experience of space and function

The form of the building is like a space craft. This building has arrived as an alien, as I did, on a friendly
mission to consolidate the town centre. I wish good fortune and calm seas to all who sail in her'.

By this time, Alsop & Lyall was established in the former substation at Alpha Place, Chelsea —
the Power House — and employing a staff of a dozen or more. Lyall's energies were particularly
directed towards the Leeds Corn Exchange project, involving the conversion of a remarkable,
Grade I listed Victorian building into a specialist shopping centre.
Work on the scheme began as early as 1984, though the revamped Exchange
was not opened until 1989. (The major change was the cutting of a large
opening into the main floor, to allow retail use to expand into the magnificent

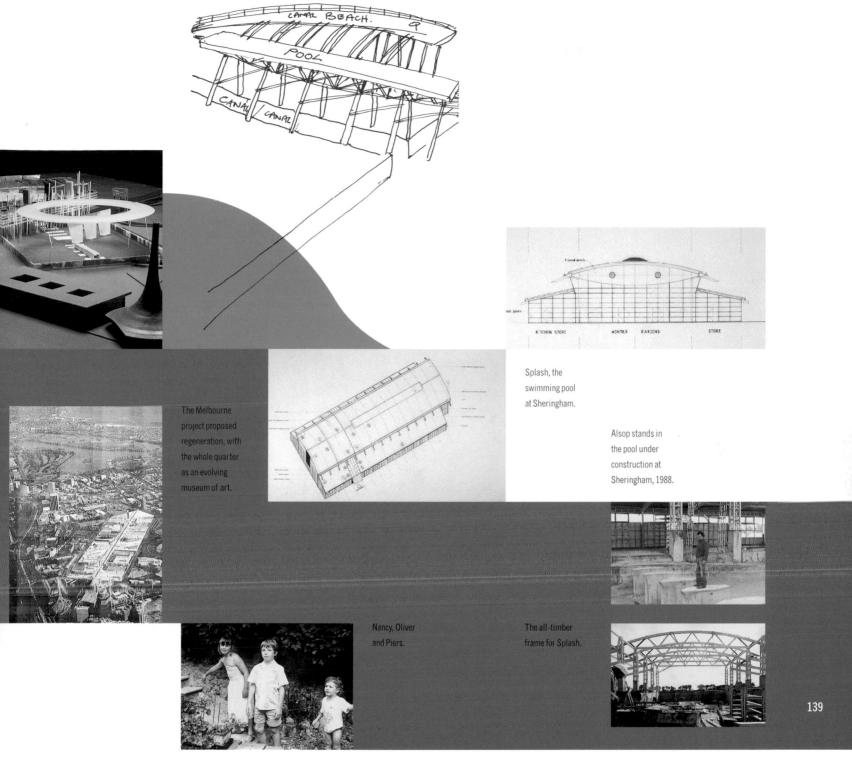

The Melbourne project proposed regeneration, with the whole quarter as an evolving museum of art.

Splash, the swimming pool at Sheringham.

Alsop stands in the pool under construction at Sheringham, 1988.

Nancy, Oliver and Piers.

The all-timber frame for Splash.

139

vaulted undercroft – there was a prolonged discussion as to how big this incision should be.) The Corn Exchange soon became the centrepiece of a dynamic, regenerated quarter of the city.

The swimming pool at Sheringham, Norfolk, was a project in which Alsop took a close personal interest. It was at Sheringham that he had bought a house (in 1984) as a weekend and holiday retreat – over the years it has become an outstation of his London office. The pool project originated with the local authority's wish to provide a 'leisure amenity' to bolster Sheringham's visitor appeal.

To achieve this objective, North Norfolk District Council decided to go into partnership with a private developer, Cliff Barnett. The idea was to provide a 'leisure pool' aimed at a family audience, with swimming as just part of the experience. Water chutes, whirlpools, a wave machine, an artificial beach and a café were to be part of the formula. This was to be a pleasure palace – an idea to which Alsop warmed – but it also had to double up as a facility for 'serious'

IT IS POSSIBLE TO ACHIEVE 18, 250 BUILDINGS IN A FIFTY-YEAR WORKING LIFE

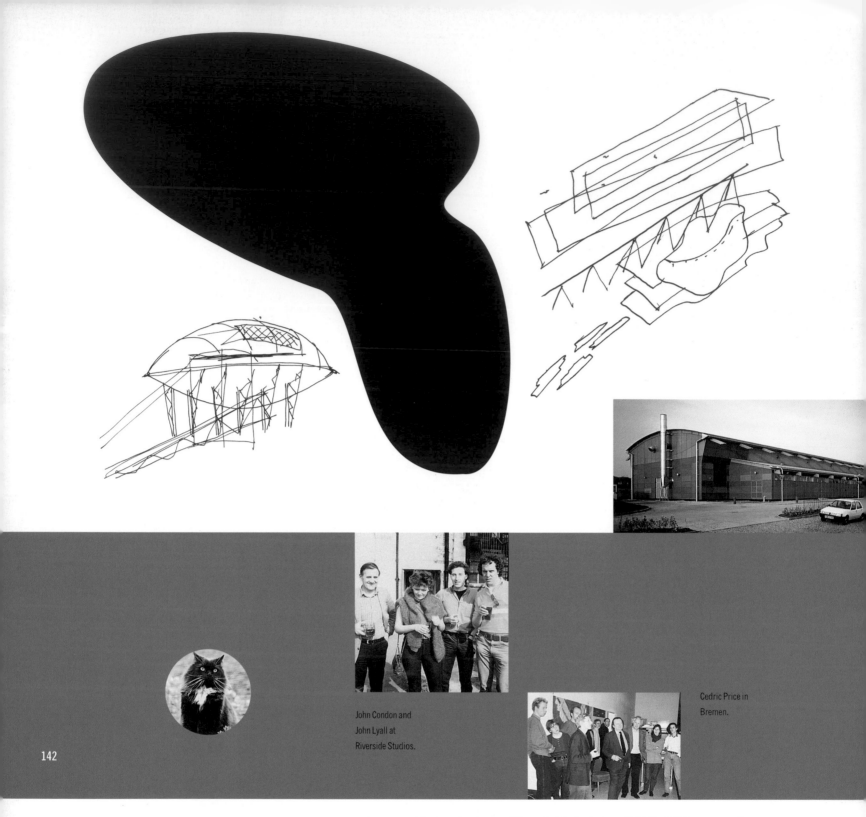

John Condon and
John Lyall at
Riverside Studios.

Cedric Price in
Bremen.

swimmers and for occasional competitions. And the budget was tight: the 3,600-square-metre-
(38,750-square-foot-) building cost just over £3 million.

'Leisure pools', usually far more costly than the Sheringham pool, had been built in many British
towns. Often the architecture was deliberately flamboyant, even kitschy – taking its cue from the
new shopping centres of booming, Thatcherite Britain. Alsop (a keen swimmer) was more attracted
by the 'straightforward' pools built by the Victorians, which he recalled from his childhood.

But these were places where people swam because they felt it was good for them – the trick at Sheringham was to combine healthy
exercise with fun. The name given to the building – Splash (thought up by Alsop's son, Oliver) – summed up the approach.

By the standards of North Norfolk, this was to be a big building – only the churches and medieval barns were on this scale. Alsop saw the
comparison as valuable – like a church, the pool should have a 'nave' where most of the action took place, with 'transepts' and 'chapels' for
more specialised activities. Externally, the pool makes no pretence of being more than a big, simple shed, clad in timber panels, its central

... the trick at Sheringham was to combine healthy exercise with fun

Splash: 'All wood is good.'

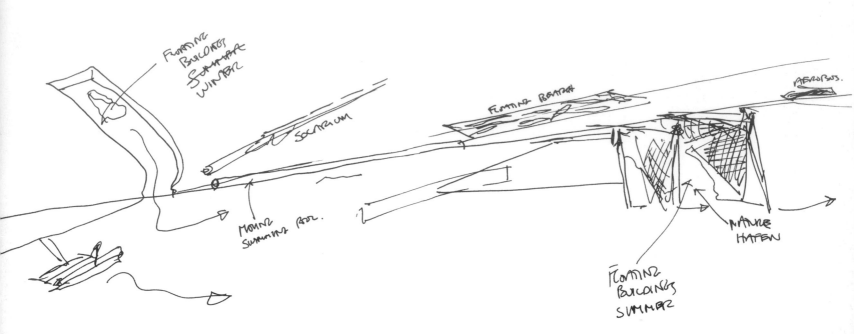

Sketches and
sketch models for
the Hafenstrasse
housing project,
Hamburg, 1988.

Opposite:
Hafenstrasse
housing project,
Hamburg.

The architect Peter
Strudwick.

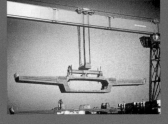

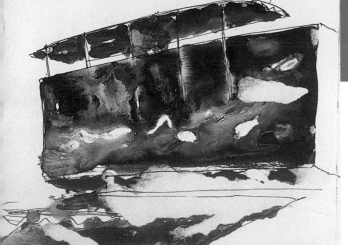

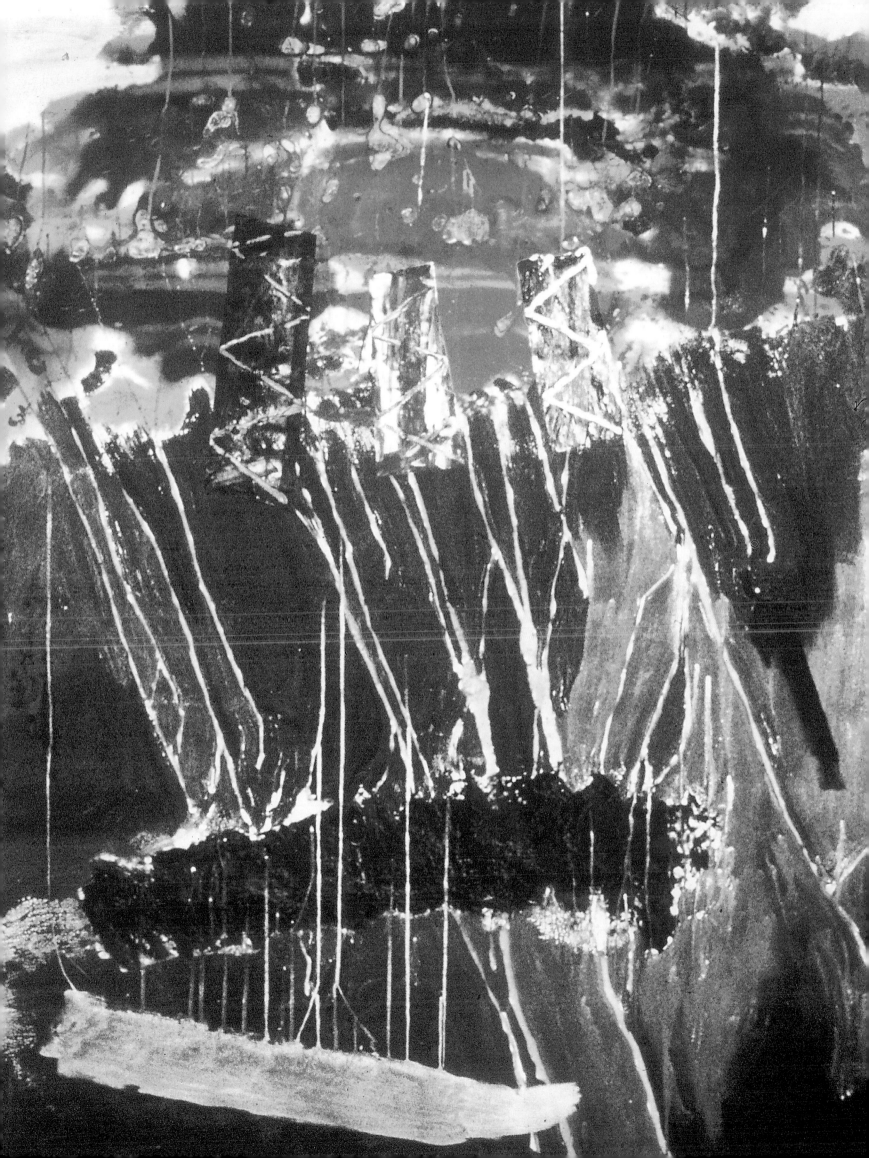

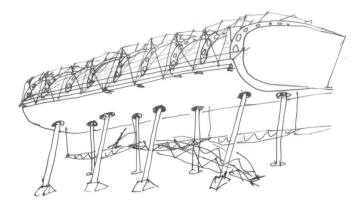

An early sketch for the Hamburg ferry terminal.

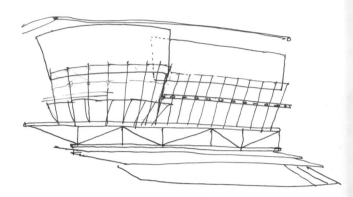

Model of
Billingsgate Pier
floating conference
centre for Citibank,
London, 1988.

Island Yard housing
project, Docklands,
London.

Waterside housing
on the Norfolk
Broads.

no style/ no beauty

Melbourne Docks
sketch, 1988.

147

'nave' flanked by subsidiary aisles. The structure, engineered by Tony Hunt, is of timber: timber lattice columns supporting laminated timber trusses. The great roof extends across the pool, a regulation 25 metres long, with attached 'beach' area for children, the winter garden and the conservatory, the latter two spaces intended to extend the use of the building as a community resource.

The cafe and bar extend along one aisle, changing rooms – actually a version of the traditional beach hut – and showers are housed in the other. For critic David Dunster, the building contained 'an imminent logic of its own'. Its architects had 'secured a new territory for architecture by taking elements of popular culture, which here is the holiday theme, and working them out using a light and ambiguous touch'.

The pool was opened by Princess Diana in 1988. Critically acclaimed, it was a major landmark in Alsop's career. It was not so much the elegance of the building that impressed as the way in which it seemed so much in tune with the users – it really was fun. This was not 'social' architecture as the AA class of 1950 would have understood it, but it was architecture which responded to people's aspirations.

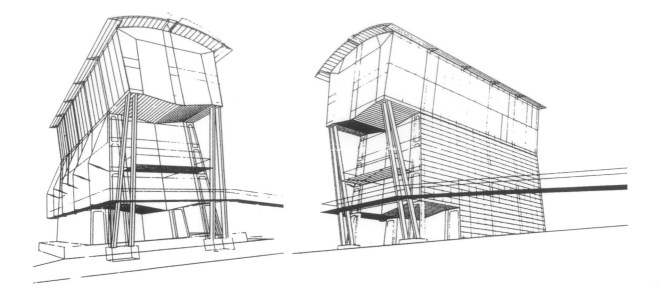

Hamburg ferry terminal (1989–93): the project evolved into a larger building after the competition.

148

Sheringham meant — and means — a lot to Alsop. He revelled in the sense of space, the big skies and the sea. For a time, he nurtured the idea of developing a career as a local architect alongside his wider activities in London and actually opened an office in Sheringham. Needless to say, things did not work out and the practice was later taken over by a former assistant, Peter Strudwick (who still runs it).

As Alsop developed his repertoire as a practitioner, the idea of landscape continued to preoccupy him just as much as it had done in his student days. Apart from Norfolk, he was intensely struck by places as diverse as Lulworth Cove in Dorset, the Australian outback and the Grand Canyon. 'Extraordinary — if an architect had designed those shapes, people would say he was mad' was Alsop's comment on the latter.

In an English farming landscape, Alsop looks at great rolls of hay and sees them as ideas for a group of buildings — both are human intrusions into nature. The landscape also exemplifies Alsop's passionate belief that 'an object can justify itself just by being beautiful'.

Opposite:
Looking south from
the Hamburg ferry
terminal hall.

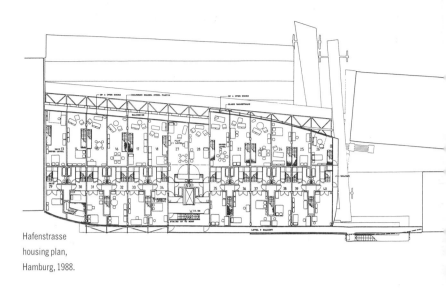

Hafenstrasse
housing plan,
Hamburg, 1988.

Hafenstrasse
section showing
how the building
copes with the two
different levels of
street frontages.

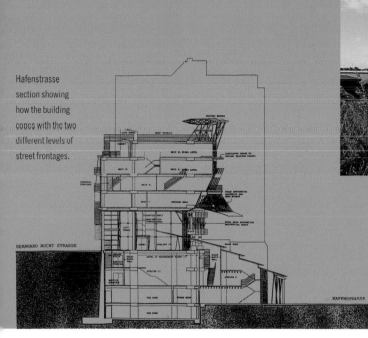

Society does not need architects to create buildings

153

Alsop's involvement in major masterplanning and infrastructure projects at the turn of the twentieth and twenty-first
centuries was prefigured by a series of commissions in the 1980s, themselves bolstered by his experiences abroad
and in Germany in particular. The Lambeth River Station (1988; see p.179) was a pier, in the same vein as the unbuilt
scheme for Westminster, but was intended not for public use but for the fire and civil defence authorities.

It was effectively a floating fire station, with crew accommodation and offices, and was fabricated
in Wales and towed to the site. The location was, however, 'sensitive' – close to Lambeth Palace
and forming part of views to the Palace of Westminster. The designs were sensibly low-key – a
simple shed, clad in profiled metal, sitting on the black painted steel substructure.

The lifting bridge at Canary Wharf (1988–91; see pp.167–8) was, on one
level, very straightforward. The bridge itself was, of course, first and
foremost an engineering structure with 25-metre (82-foot) spans for each of
its components. The architects' input was concentrated on the control
building, which became a highly sculptural object, with a control cabin

Family hotel, Island
Yard, Docklands,
London.

... an object can justify itself just by being beautiful

The Shopping
Centre at Hérouville
Saint-Clair flies in.

Alsop on his fortieth
birthday.

cantilevered off the main structure to provide maximum visibility.
The building was made of welded steel plate – like a ship. 'It was the
first project where I was involved with civil engineers', says Alsop. The
project involved discussions with Canary Wharf's US-based masterplanners
and Alsop recalls being dismayed by the fact that every move had to be
referred back to Chicago for a decision.

The station at Tottenham Hale was far more significant and undoubtedly paved the way for Alsop's work on the Jubilee Line Extension, CrossRail and
Thameslink 2000. The station was a convenient point of connection between suburban services out of London Liverpool Street and the Underground's Victoria
Line, opened in the late Sixties. Its significance was, however, greatly boosted by the major expansion plans for Stansted airport, first developed as a wartime
bomber base, as 'London's third airport' – Norman Foster's new terminal at Stansted opened in 1991 – with its fast rail link to London.

It was decided to rebuild Tottenham Hale's extremely mean Victorian station to cope with a
much expanded traffic. Logically, the rebuilding had to include both surface and Underground

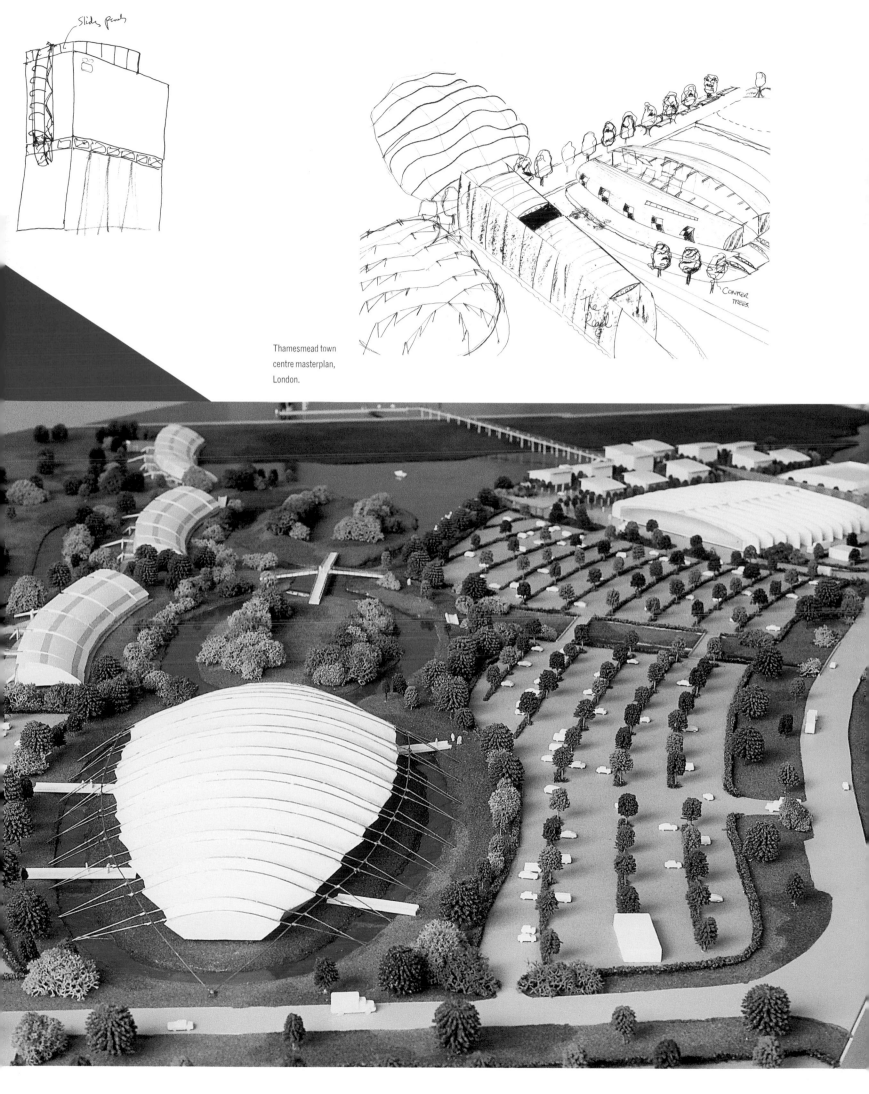

Thamesmead town
centre masterplan,
London.

Images for a Realworld project in Barcelona.

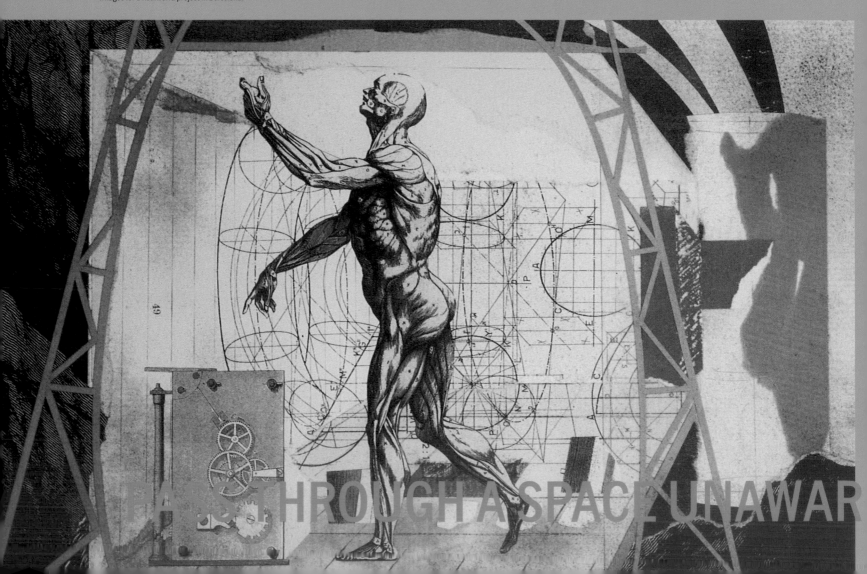

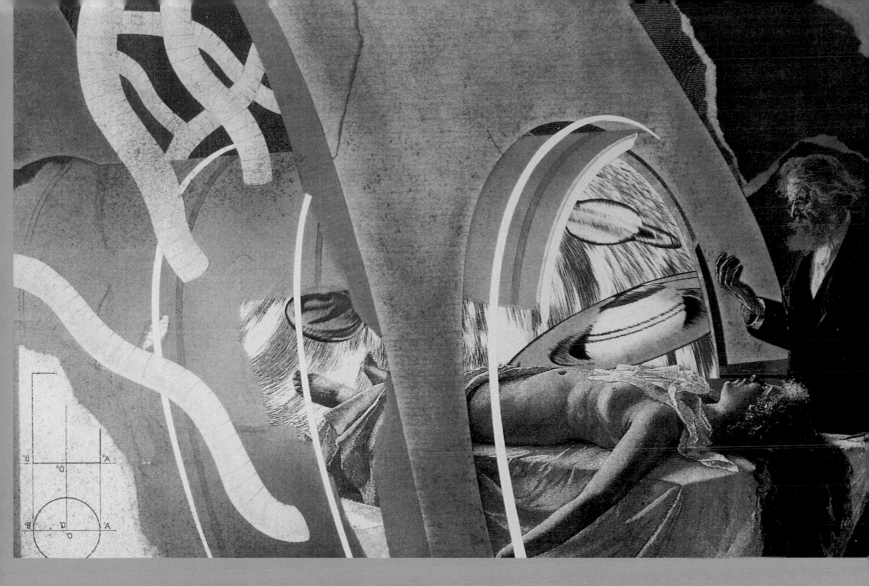

OF ARRIVAL OR DEPARTURE

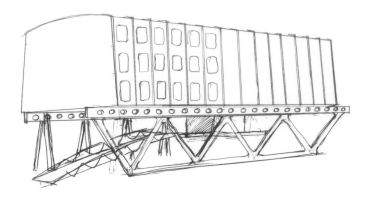

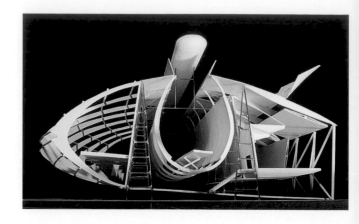

Proposal for the
British Pavilion for
Seville Expo '92,
Alsop's first foray
into low-energy
architecture.

Overleaf:
Sketch for the
British Pavillion,
Seville Expo '92.

Hôtel du
Département.
Sketch made for the
second stage of
the competition.

The first stage
submission for
the Hôtel du
Département
competition,
Marseilles: just one
entry out of 150.

159

stations but initially only the surface station was tackled, with British Rail as client and a
very modest budget of £2 million. The brief was for a new waiting room, ticket office and
station canopy, no more (see pp.180–85).

Tottenham Hale was an instructive project for Alsop, stimulating an exploration of ends and means within the context
of a parsimonious budget. For a time, there was the idea of putting a lightweight fabric structure over the station, but it
was dropped – impermanence is not part of the vocabulary of railways. The imperative for economy was, to some
degree, counterbalanced by the interest of the local authority in making the station a beacon of regeneration in a drab
area. It was this that led to the creation of what was claimed as 'the longest double-sided art work in the world'.

Painting was, by this time, a regular element in Alsop's working method. (He tends to paint mainly at Sheringham,
working long hours in the simple studio which he built for himself in the garden, or during summer holidays in another
favourite spot, Minorca.) Bringing together artists and architects and ending the divorce between art and architecture

THE EMPLOYMENT AND ENJOYMENT OF THOSE MAKIN

BUILDING IS A JUSTIFICATION IN ITS OWN RIGHT

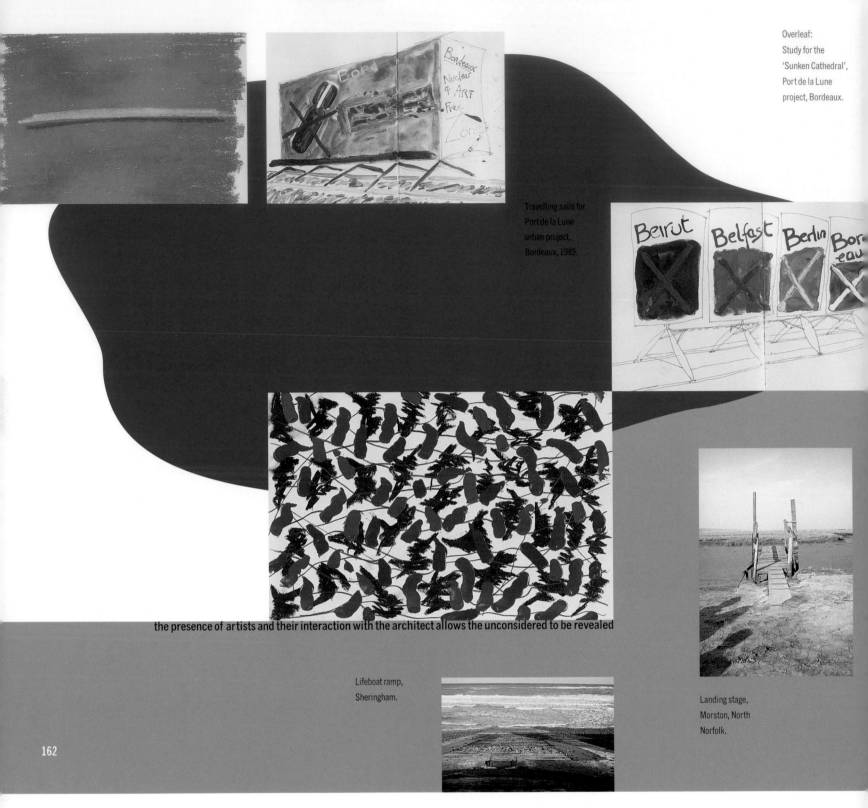

Overleaf:
Study for the
'Sunken Cathedral',
Port de la Lune
project, Bordeaux.

Travelling sails for
Port de la Lune
urban project,
Bordeaux, 1989.

Beirut   Belfast   Berlin   Bor
eau

the presence of artists and their interaction with the architect allows the unconsidered to be revealed

Lifeboat ramp,
Sheringham.

Landing stage,
Morston, North
Norfolk.

162

which was supposedly one of the less happy products of the Modern Movement is an objective which is incontestably worthy. It is often presented as a matter of re-connecting a natural union, evident in every fine building from the Parthenon to the Glasgow Art School, which was arbitrarily broken off sometime around 1920.

Unfortunately, the results are often clumsy and banal — too often the art is applied as a palliative, to mitigate the negative impact of the architecture. (In the 1960s, for example, it was quite common for sculpture, often by eminent artists, to be attached to mundane offices and department stores, to indicate presumably that the developers were not without some taste.) Alsop argues that, for the collaboration to work, it must be a matter of seamless integration: 'the prime requirement is a mutual respect, an established friendship and a discreet flexibility — to avoid the question of what the individual role is'.

He continues: 'the presence of artists and their interaction with the architect allows the unconsidered to be revealed and prevents the use of precedent and style being utilised as a justification for a proposal. I do not believe that our task is concerned with the re-interpretation of the familiar for the peace of mind of the user, but more with the enjoyment of the unexpected. Style has always been a part of architecture, but not of art. The art of manners is essentially concerned with the degree of attentiveness; mere re-interpretation is inattentive and sometimes rude.'

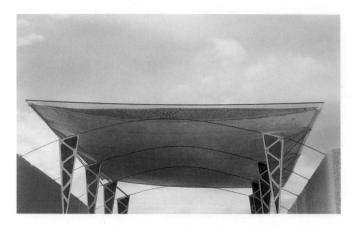

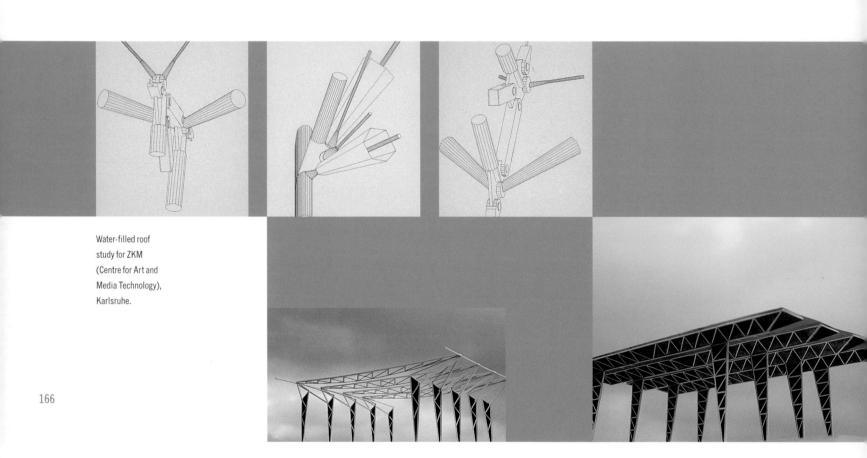

Water-filled roof study for ZKM (Centre for Art and Media Technology), Karlsruhe.

166

It is an advantage, argues Alsop, that 'on the whole, artists lack taste' – they are uncontaminated by the precedent-based training of the architect (which leads to architects perceiving themselves as part of schools or movements – High-tech, Post Modernist, Deconstructivist…) and can help him towards work which is uncompromising, maybe ugly, but certainly not contained within the stifling bounds of 'good taste'.

Alsop dismisses the idea that artists should be confined to embellishing a scheme – 'architecture must become the artist's medium'.

These ideas are central to Alsop's philosophy of architecture. The idea of an architect choosing a single style in which to design is for him abhorrent – it is like choosing a suit of clothes and wearing it day in, day out.

One alternative is the 'pluralism' which leads to architects offering clients a choice of stylings for their buildings – that is, façadism. Philip Johnson pioneered this thinking. In the 1980s, it flourished, so that an office building on Ludgate Hill in London, on the processional route to St Paul's, was clad in panellised Classical details in order that the Prince of Wales, en route to state occasions, would not be offended by the sight of modern architecture. For Alsop, this is reducing architecture to 'image making… a game of surface stylistics'.

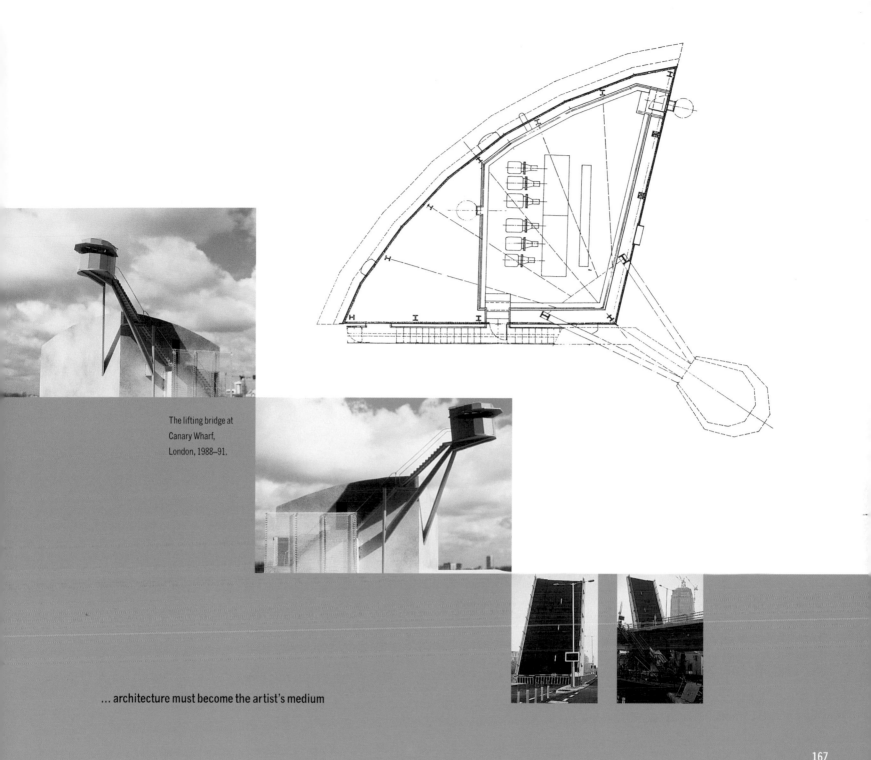

The lifting bridge at Canary Wharf, London, 1988–91.

... architecture must become the artist's medium

Alsop's motto, 'no style/ no beauty', does not imply that he sees his work as deliberately styleless or lacking in beauty, not even that he dismisses the idea of 'image making' – a building should make an impression on those who see it – 'by making a building you are contributing to people's lives', Alsop insists.

What Alsop rejects is the idea that style is something applied, a facile coating – it is, for him, the very essence of architecture and the outcome of a hard creative process, not a matter of picking a garment off a rail. The Saxon builders who designed the tower of Earls Barton church (see p.9), which Alsop discovered as a child and vastly admired, understood that. Mel Gooding has written of Alsop's 'humane practicality', insisting that 'Alsop is no theorist. His philosophy is provisional and non-prescriptive, the evolving and dynamic outcome of creative collaborations and actual problem solving'.

The dynamic tension between practicality and ideals was strongly felt at Tottenham Hale. On the practical level, the station was given a striking new glazed frontage, with an elegant steel and

Early sketch for
Cardiff Bay
barrage.

… by making a building you are contributing to people's lives

glass footbridge linking the platforms, and a curved passenger building (with waiting room and buffet), like a moored ship, complete with portholes, or a parked bus. A long strip of the frontage was, however, filled with a painting by Bruce McLean – 'it was as cheap as filling it with glass', says Alsop. The effect of the intervention was, however, to make mundane Tottenham Hale a special, distinctive place.

It is certainly a building which makes an impact on the public domain and represents Alsop's far from tentative response to Cedric Price's rhetorical question 'why not?'. Why should a transport building assume a 'functional' look? Assuming that the practical requirements of the brief are met, can it not also contain an element of delight, of the extraordinary?

Alsop's architecture does not spurn practical issues, but, having addressed them, moves on to consider issues beyond those of practicality. In its realisation, there is often a clear expression of practical 'bones' (the structure of a building) underlying the flesh of architectural expression. At heart, Alsop is a pragmatist, of a sort, in the British tradition, but he refuses to countenance the

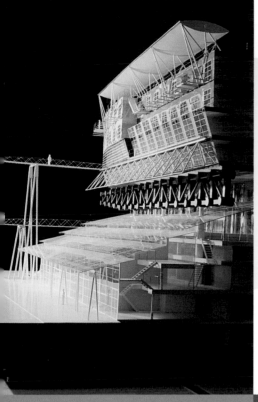

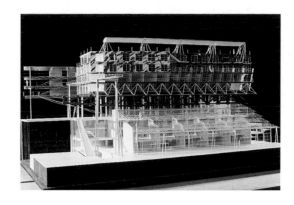

Model for
Hafenstrasse,
Hamburg, a mixed
development of
housing and
workshops, 1988.

169

Sketches and
sketch models for
the Cardiff Bay
barrage, 1990.

HOME SITE

ALSO WATER PERFORMANCE

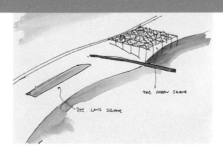

PALE LAND SQUARE

PALE GREEN SQUARE

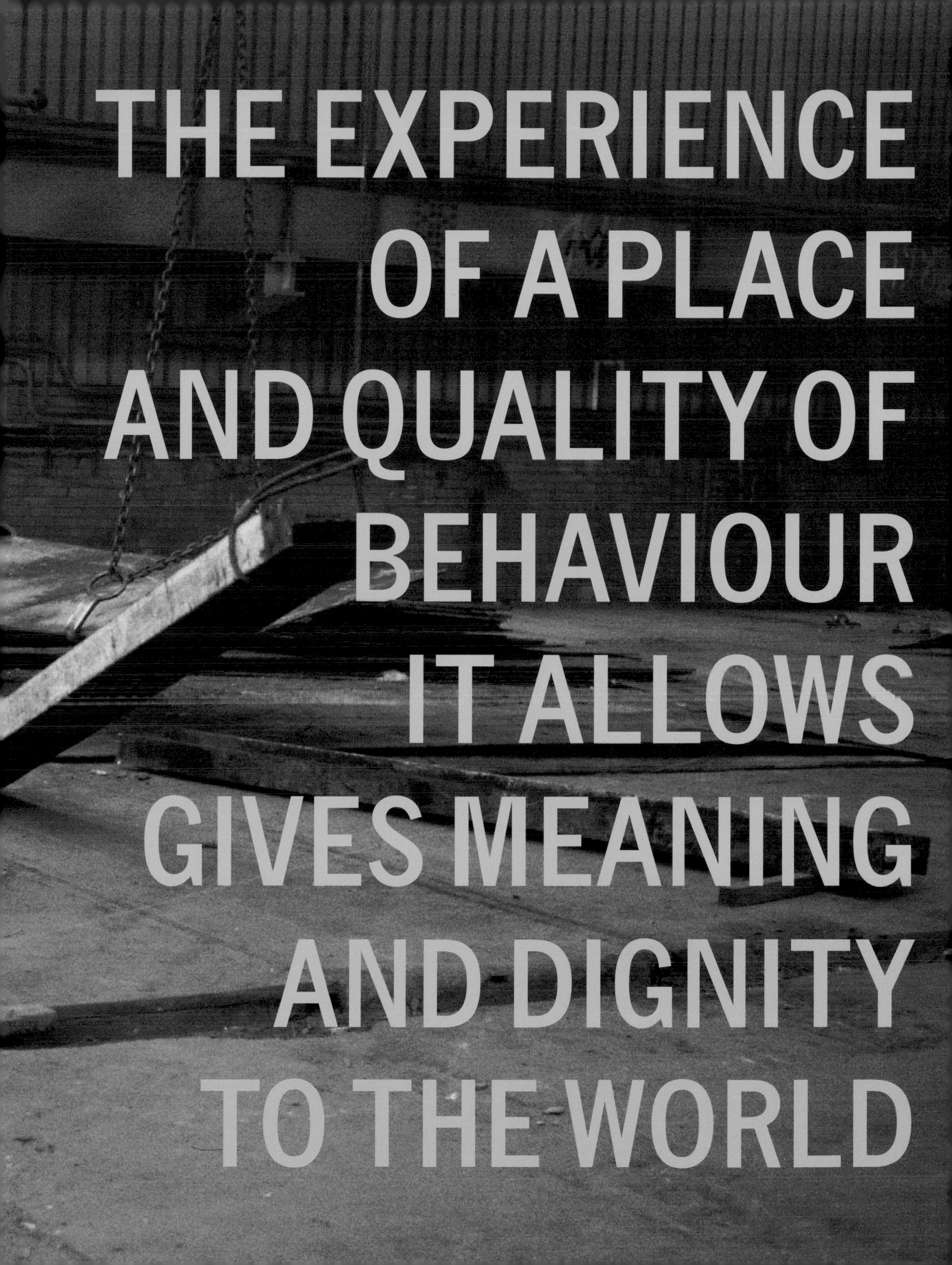

THE EXPERIENCE
OF A PLACE
AND QUALITY OF
BEHAVIOUR
IT ALLOWS
GIVES MEANING
AND DIGNITY
TO THE WORLD

Alsop's office at
Bremen Academy of
Art and Music.

View of the Albert
Bridge from Alsop's
first Battersea
office, London.

idea that looking beyond function makes you impractical, a mere dreamer – was Isambard
Kingdom Brunel, a visionary if ever there was one, an impractical man?

As Alsop moved from being thirty-something to forty-something, his architecture responded, in its boldness and
confidence, to the challenge of creating real buildings. It was during the later Eighties that the partnership of Alsop
and Lyall began to come under pressure – it was eventually dissolved in 1991 – and the distinct approaches of the two
partners to emerge more clearly.

Alsop's interests and ambitions had assumed an unequivocally international dimension which extended beyond
Europe. His enthusiasm for Australia had led to several projects in Melbourne, including a scheme for the city's
Museum of Contemporary Art (see pp.138–9).
Alsop's idea for an 'evolutionary' museum included the idea of galleries with a series of car showrooms (as enabling
commercial development) on top – 'a very Australian notion'. An ambitious masterplan (1988) for Melbourne's

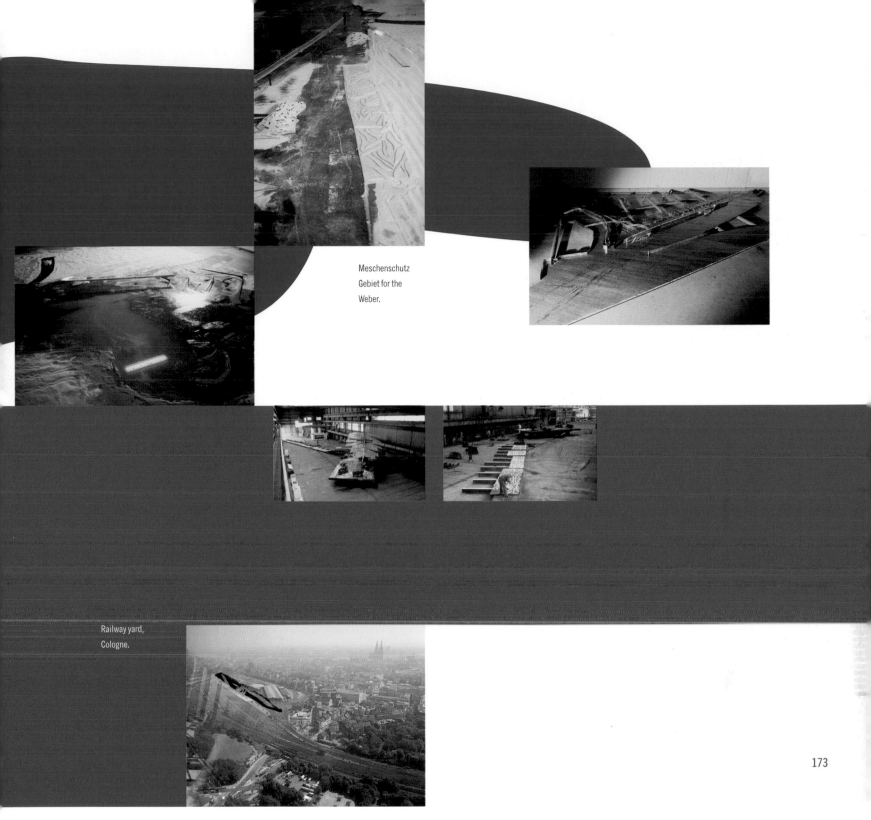

Meschenschutz
Gebiet for the
Weber.

Railway yard,
Cologne.

decayed docklands produced ideas for a development which focused on the issue of movement. A system of cranes allowed spaces to be freely reconfigured to suit changing needs – there were strong echoes of Cedric Price's Interaction. But the most important issue in Melbourne was that of connecting the port area to the centre of the city, giving more people access to water close to the heart of Melbourne, thus allowing local people 'to experience and participate in a rich variety of physical entities, which can be mixed in unexpected ways.

The richness of experience gives meaning to the city'. Ports and harbours, and the relationship between cities and waterfronts, was becoming a constant theme in Alsop's work. It was to be further extended in his work in Cardiff.

Alsop's involvement with Cardiff Bay (where Lyall was, fortuitously, also to work after the dissolution of the practice) came about as a result of the establishment of the Cardiff Bay Development Corporation. The CBDC was one of a number of such bodies set up, at the instigation of Tory Environment Secretary Michael Heseltine, to regenerate depressed areas in and around the major cities.

In Cardiff, as in London, Liverpool and Bristol, the focus was on the former docklands. Cardiff had once been the largest coal port in the world, but, with the coal trade gone, the docks area faced a crisis. The CBDC's strategy was to

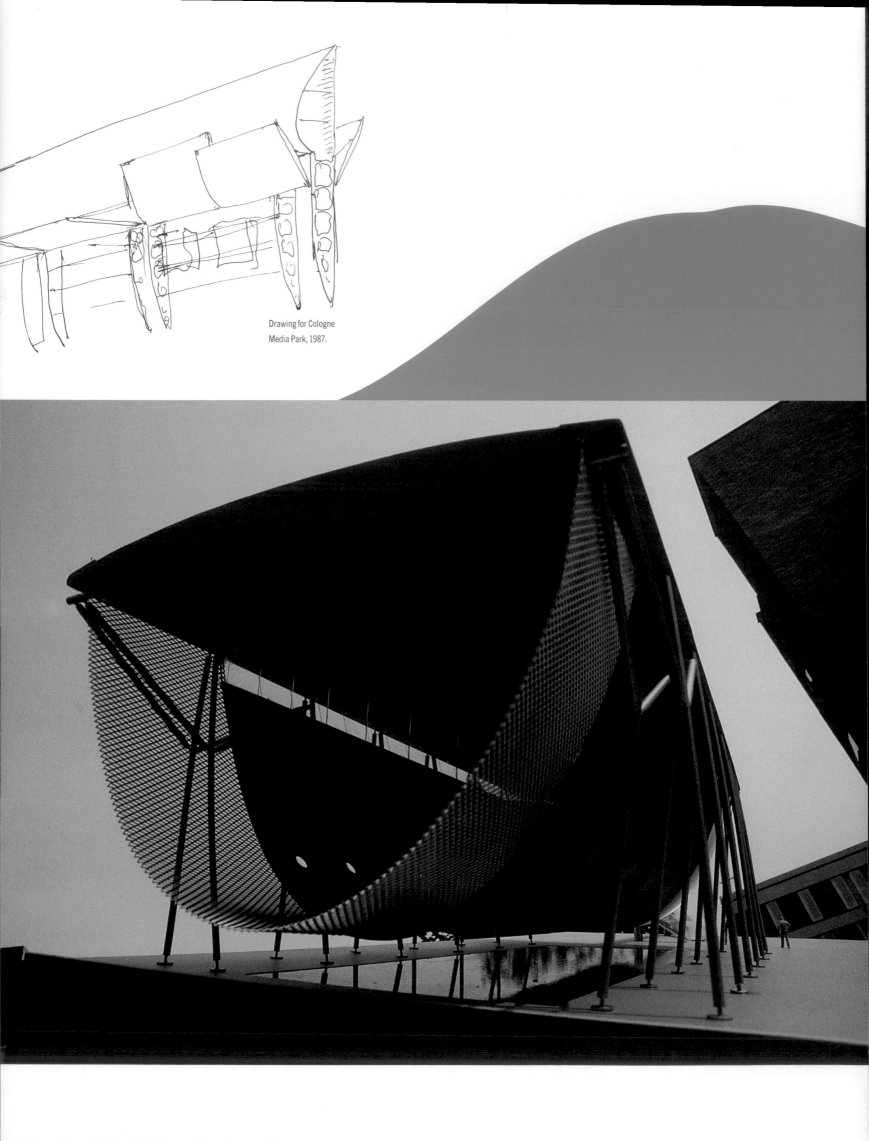

Drawing for Cologne
Media Park, 1987.

Proposal for
Templemeads
Visitor Centre,
Bristol, 1991.

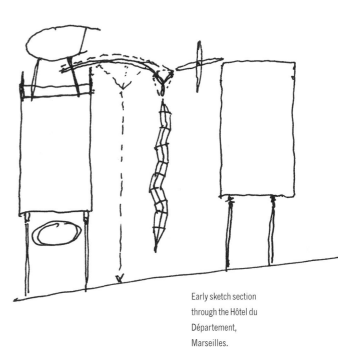

Early sketch section
through the Hôtel du
Département,
Marseilles.

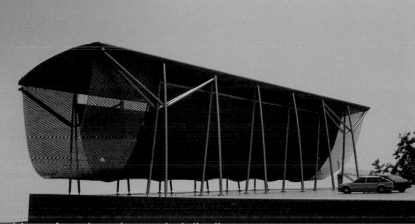

The richness of experience gives meaning to the city

Garden studio,
Sheringham.

attract new office development into the area and equally to develop the docklands as an attractive visitor location, with hotels, bars and restaurants around the Pierhead (a mile distant from the centre of the city). Central to this strategy was the Cardiff Bay Barrage, which extends across the mouth of the bay, creating a freshwater lake into which the rivers Taff and Ely drain – the aim was to make an expanse of water which looked appealing and was ideal for sailing and other sports.

Alsop was to be heavily involved with the Barrage for nearly a decade (1990–99), transforming what could have been a piece of functional engineering into a *Gesamtkunstwerk*, but his first Cardiff project was the 'temporary' (it is still standing) visitor centre which was erected in five months in the summer of 1990, at a cost of £350,000. It was shortlisted for the RIBA's Building of the Year award – the forerunner to the Stirling Prize (see pp.188–93).

The Cardiff visitor centre was designed to contain displays relating to the CBDC's plans and to document the progress of regeneration in the docklands. The most obvious feature of the building is its strong and memorable form – some have likened it to a Swiss roll, while, for

Workshop at
Hamburg for
Spiecher Stadt.

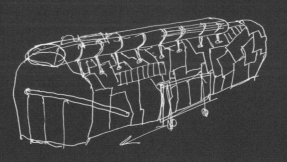

Floating carrots.

Alsop, it resembles a disposable cigarette lighter. 'It's a corrective to the idea that you have to agonise endlessly over the form of a building', he says.

Given the short life span of the centre, context was not seen as a prime issue – though the site was close to the large and ornate late Victorian Pierhead Building. (The RIBA's awards committee was later to commend the centre for creating its own context.) In essence, the structure was very simple: a series of oval steel ribs support a cladding of marine plywood panelling. Abstract shapes cut into the cladding provide an element of dappled daylight inside. A layer of PVC sheeting stretched over the entire structure protects it from the weather.

The centre is in the tradition of lightweight, portable structures which was so strong at the AA during Alsop's time there. Like one of Archigram's fantastic structures, it uprooted itself and walked – or rather was carried on a low-loader – when the CBDC decided to move it a few hundred yards. There was a real possibility, in fact, that the building would be permanently dismantled.

Floating fire station,
Lambeth, London
(made in Wales),
1990.

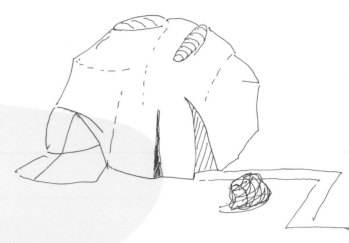

179

This caused something of a furore — it had already become a popular landmark — and the decision was therefore made to relocate it. (The irony of the controversy became apparent when, firstly, Alsop's Swansea Literature Centre was cancelled and later Zaha Hadid's Cardiff opera house also fell victim to a campaign of opposition whipped up by the local media.)

Alsop was delighted at the public's liking for the centre. Since the days at the AA, when he had sympathised with the campaigning ideas of community activists like Brian Anson and Jim Monahan, Alsop's ideas on public participation had developed and matured.

For architects of an older generation, such ideas were highly heterodox — the normal democratic process was enough and it was up to central and local government to decide what was built and where.

This was the basis on which Britain had been recast in the 1950s and 1960s. For a younger generation of architects, born since the Second World War, the heroic ideals of the recent past did not seem to be reflected in humdrum city centres and bleak housing estates.

Tottenham Hale
station, with Bruce
McLean's mural,
1991.

Opposite:
Detail of a porthole
window at
Tottenham Hale.

In Cedric Price's office, Alsop had been immersed in a radical, even subversive ambience – Price
saw the architect as an agent of change, making a better life for everyone. The social agenda
behind a building project was what mattered, not the look of the building.

Art hardly entered into the equation. At this point, Alsop begged to differ. The delight (the 'wow factor') which people get from the
Cardiff Bay visitor centre, the Peckham Library or North Greenwich station matters for Alsop. Ultimately, an architect, like a sculptor
or painter, makes arbitrary decisions. Architecture achieves built form at the point where individual creativity and the collective
consciousness collide.

For some critics, there is a disturbing conflict between Alsop's avowed commitment to community involvement and an
approach to architecture which is frankly artistic, concerned with the creation of bold form. There does not seem to be
much scope for participation in Alsop's work. 'Architecture is a conformist art', he admits.

'Architects can only achieve things because society/politicians/developers let them'. Some of the greatest projects
in history – those of Etienne Boullée or Claude-Nicolas Ledoux, for example, of the Russian Constructivists or of

a modern hero like Frederick Kiessler – are fated to remain unbuilt. Not that the architecture of ideas is in any way less significant than that of steel, brick and concrete. Society does not need architects to create buildings – most buildings are not designed by architects. The role of the architect lies beyond the fact of construction.

In developing his own approach to 'community architecture', Alsop has been conscious of the natural tension between consensus and innovation – it is only by fully involving people in architectural projects, rather than presenting a developed scheme to them and asking for comments in a sort of referendum, that it can become a creative force rather than a purely negative or reactionary one. Compromise and consensus can destroy creative art.

The public, along with the client and the critical community, should be part of the debate about a proposed building. (Alsop's view of critics is uncompromising: 'the architectural critic is often the lowest form of architectural and intellectual life, as they feed on the placing of constraints on the work of the architect. Good critics become collaborators and as such contribute to the body of ideas that will help us to replace a little of the misery in the world with a little joy and delight'.)

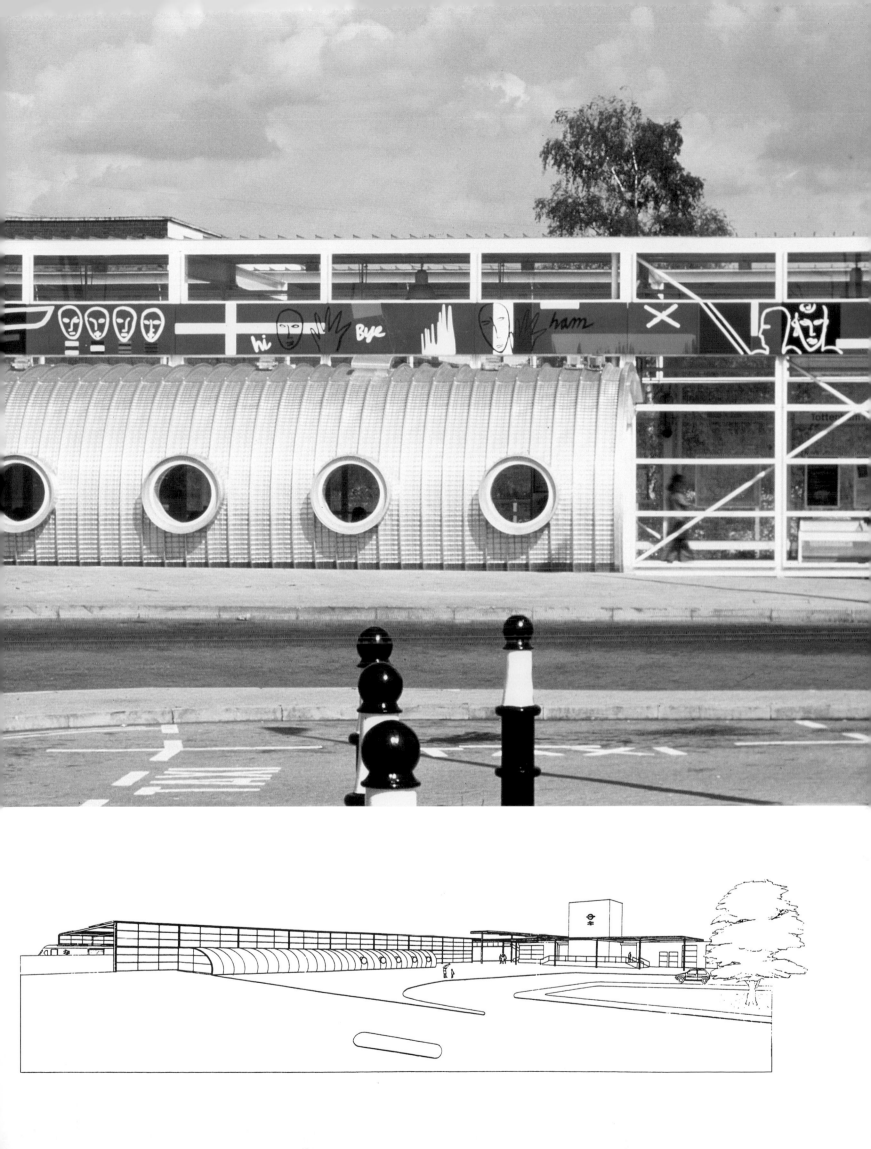

The social agenda behind a building project was what mattered, not the look of the building.

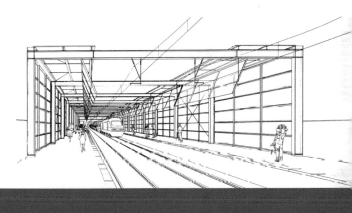

The old station at
Tottenham Hale.

Alsop's early preoccupation with landscape was, in part, a response to the
post-Sixties mood of disillusionment with architecture. 'My initial response
to the public disgust at the buildings that the majority of architects produce
was to find ways of making them invisible.
It therefore followed that landscape allowed me to exercise my desires to manipulate objects and space and remain invisible as recognisable buildings.
I was struck by the concept of people being able to pass through a place without having known that they had either arrived or left it'.

Natural landscape is part of the context of a building, but so, insists Alsop, is the human landscape — 'the people who
live adjacent to, and work or visit an area, as as much a part of the 'context' as anything else'... Earlier generations of
modern architects had looked to political and economic theories (and later to sociology) to guide their social response.
For Alsop, human behaviour is not such an exact science. Designing buildings to reflect supposedly fixed patterns of living
is a dangerous game: shouldn't a building be able to respond to the unpredictability of human life and emotions? Alsop
once designed 'a house for a day' — for him, there is nothing absurd about the idea. Why should one day replicate another?

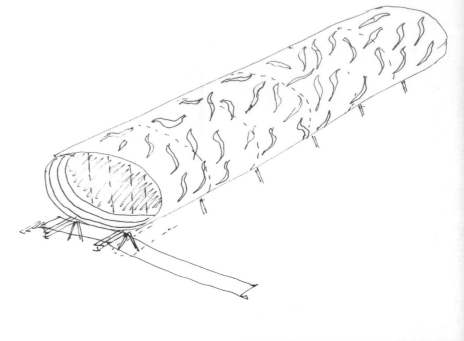

Cigarette lighter as
building (Cardiff
Bay Visitor Centre).

It's a corrective to the idea that you have to agonise endlessly over the form of a building.

'You don't start with a fully designed building, then get people in to approve (or disapprove)', says Alsop of his approach to participation.
'Your starting point should be the whole community of interested persons. You need to harness the power, the imagination that is latent in
those people, welding it to the imagination and skills that we, as architects, hopefully possess'.

Reinventing 'community architecture' means making it something different from the definition which the Prince of
Wales promoted in the 1980s. 'We all want to make life better, I assume. All architecture is social in that it affects
people's lives. Getting it right isn't easy: it's hard work and we're only gradually learning how to set about it'.

Alsop was greatly influenced by his experience of the Hamburg Bauforum. But it is not just a matter of talking. Alsop
has been an active teacher throughout his career – at St Martin's, the AA, in the USA, Germany and, latterly, Vienna.
His classes are no-holds-barred occasions – workshops extend late into the night, an extraordinary range of
materials, from cardboard to chicken wire, is brought to bear, there are no rules. Such is the vacuum in architecture,
says Alsop, that we need to unleash the imagination to attempt to fill it. This is the key to the new community
architecture. 'If people really feel that they have a stake in a project, that their ideas count, they can be amazingly bold,

Cardiff Bay Visitor
Centre under
construction.

Your starting point should be the whole community of interested persons

189

contemplating extraordinary ideas that they might otherwise have dismissed as impractical, outlandish. Alsop's idea
of a public consultation is not sitting people in rows and lecturing to them, then asking them for comments.

'I believe in less talking, more drawing and painting', he says. 'Get people to sit down and show you the way they see a
building, work with them, develop the ideas, show them yours. Design is an exploratory process, like painting. As you
work, the concept emerges — you must not come with a preconception of the way it should look'.

In recent projects, such as C-Plex at West Bromwich and the community centre for the Stonebridge Park housing estate, Alsop & Störmer brought these ideas to
bear and, in the process, as Alsop admits, the practice's own ideas on community and participation developed and matured. Alsop's own, once-tentative faith in
participation has become very much a core belief.

Winning the competition for the Hôtel du Département des Bouches-du-Rhône in Marseilles in 1990 was a clear watershed in Will Alsop's
career. It led to the break-up of the partnership with Lyall and the formation of a new international practice of Alsop & Störmer with Jan
Störmer, formerly a partner in Hamburg's MeDiUm practice. Alsop's scheme won through over a field of 156 entries and triumphed in a
run-off with the legendarily unbeatable Norman Foster.

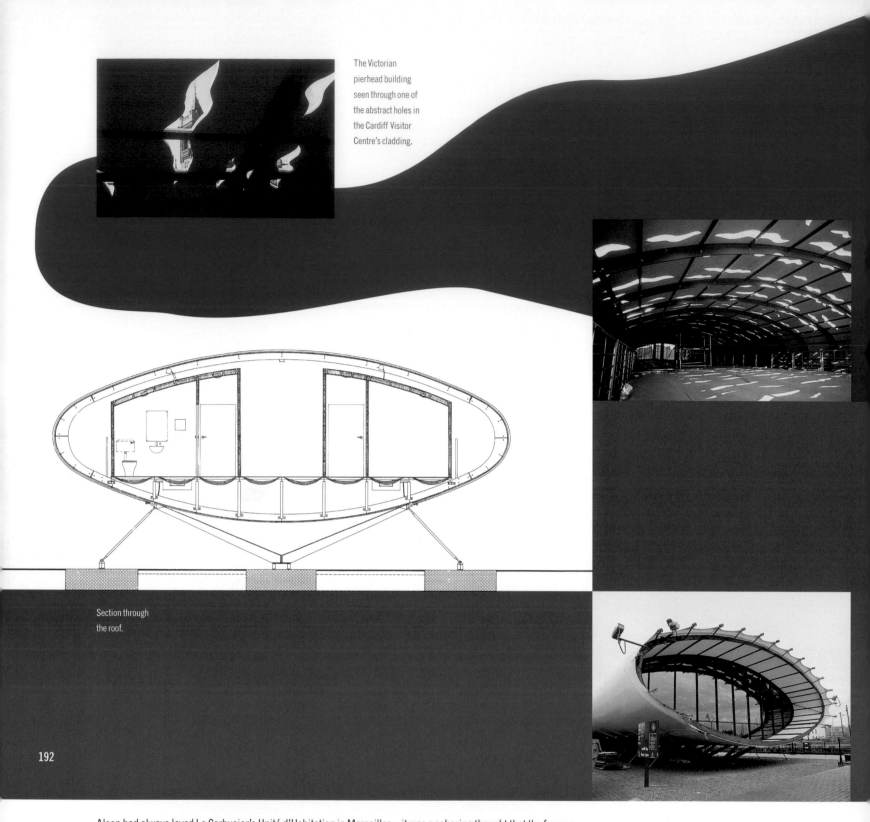

The Victorian
pierhead building
seen through one of
the abstract holes in
the Cardiff Visitor
Centre's cladding.

Section through
the roof.

Alsop had always loved Le Corbusier's Unité d'Habitation in Marseilles – it was a sobering thought that the famous
modernist monument could sit comfortably within the atrium of Alsop's building. 'It was my admiration for the Unité
which convinced me that I had to enter the Marseilles competition', Alsop recalls.

In designing what could cynically be seen as a palace for bureaucrats, Alsop had the idea of an 'open' building – 'the
building will create an impression with the citizens, not because of its monumentality, but because the building invites
you to enter it. My building will settle into the area without any ambition to dominate it'.

The siting of the Hôtel du Département was, like the Cardiff Bay Barrage and the proposed Hérouville Tower, a political gesture, with
regeneration as its principal engine. The building was to be sited outside the centre of Marseilles and the influence of the municipal
administration, in the St Just area. It was easily accessible by the local metro system (indeed, Alsop's building straddles the tracks).

The Marseilles project – the Grand Bleu, as this gigantic piece of urban sculpture was to become
known – launched Alsop's career in the top league of European architects, but it was equally the

realisation of ideas which he had developed over the previous 25 years. In simple terms, the
scheme as built consists of two slabs of offices flanking a full-height, daylit atrium. To one side
lies the separate Deliberatif block, with the 'squashed cigar' form seen in the Cardiff Visitor
Centre and containing council chamber and committee rooms, plus an element of flexible space
which can be tailored to accommodate a range of meetings and events (see pp.196–202).

'Exciting, comfortable and approachable' were the adjectives which Alsop hoped to see applied to the building. The practical strengths of Alsop's competition
entry were its commitment to low-energy design, and successful response to the unpredictable climatic conditions of the French south, and its use of
commonplace materials – concrete, glass, steel – to produce a tough and durable building at a moderate cost. (It was built in little more than two years.)

Underlying the physical form of the building there was, however, a powerful idea of how it might be used and enjoyed.
Alsop envisaged a building with 'good places to sit, to drink coffee, or buy a newspaper. The idea here is to give
comfort to visitors and employees in a volume of great spatial excitement. The area will be cool, comfortable…
The space is a public forum for discussion and delight'. The great central atrium is the realisation of this vision of

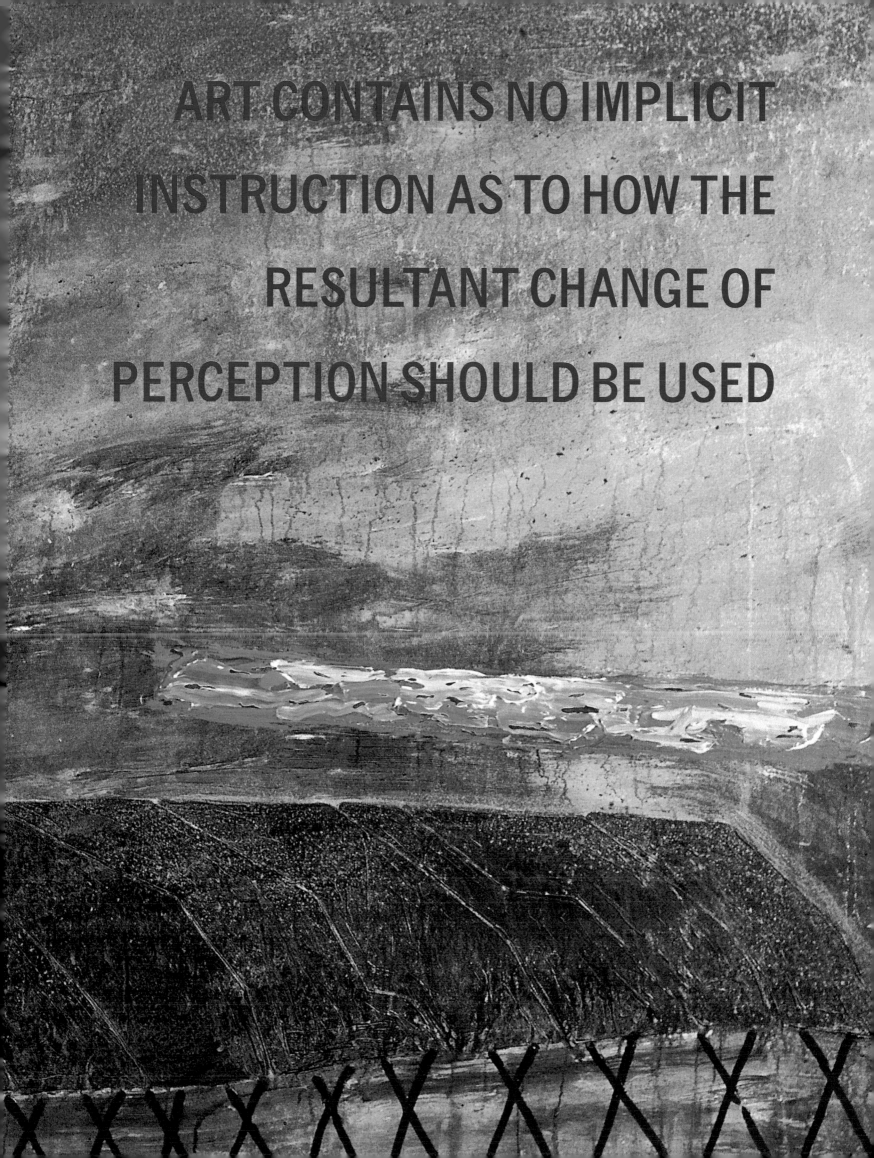

ART CONTAINS NO IMPLICIT INSTRUCTION AS TO HOW THE RESULTANT CHANGE OF PERCEPTION SHOULD BE USED

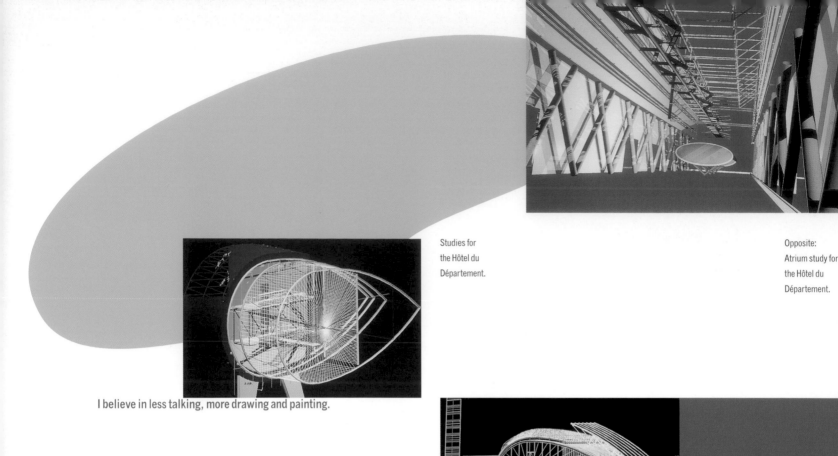

Studies for
the Hôtel du
Département.

Opposite:
Atrium study for
the Hôtel du
Département.

I believe in less talking, more drawing and painting.

Roof study for the
metro entrance for
the Hôtel du
Département.

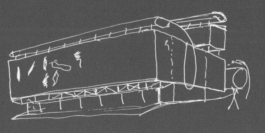

196

bureaucracy humanised by contact with the outside world. With its linking bridges, from which civil servants get an exciting, if vertiginous, view of the public arena below, this is one of the great spaces of post-war European architecture. But it is the interaction between building and user which gives the building its special magic.

Recording his thoughts on a visit to Hannover in 1990, Alsop mused on the role of the architect. 'The obsession with style and beauty' concerned him – 'we know that all the great work of architects of former generations is much loved. This love creates a huge number of patches on the Earth's surface which cannot be built on.
The work of our forefathers clogs up the possibility of changing patterns of life…
It is perhaps our responsibility not to create buildings that people fall in love with'.

On the verge of his breakthrough into international success and celebrity, Alsop remained a radical, a sceptic, someone who questioned orthodoxies, defied rules and didn't easily 'fit' into a British scene still dominated by High-tech and Post-Modernism. With its stress on the user and

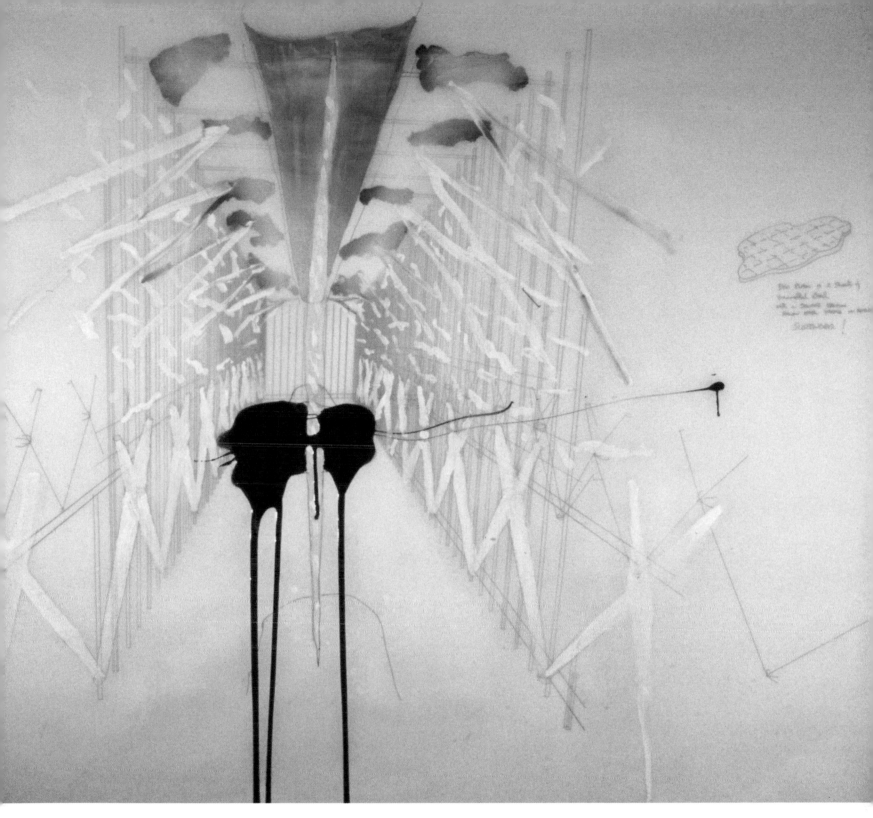

on buildings which responded to, rather than predicated, human lifestyles, its commitment to flexibility and freedom and its colourful expressiveness, Alsop's architecture reflected its roots in the years of experimentation at the AA — the birthplace of 'pluralism' — and in that era of social ferment which had culminated in the youth revolt of 1968. There was also a strong belief in architecture as art, rather than technology — in the role of the architect to make forms, to create, not just echo technical and functional formulae. Alsop's shapes looked outrageously novel to anyone raised on a diet of engineering-based High-tech buildings.

Yet beneath the surface, Alsop's work had a clear structural rationale — Marseilles demonstrated the highly practical nature of his vision. Where Alsop innovated was in his refusal to allow structure and services to mould form.
He sees engineering as a means to an end, and services as a way of making buildings comfortable and useable, not a set of jewels to be put on display

Opposite:
Looking towards
Marseilles and
the future.

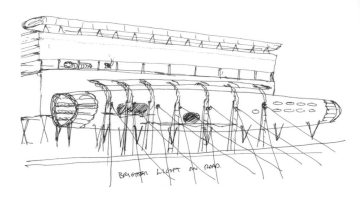

Alsop with Pierre
Garnier, Chief
Architect for the
Département des
Bouches du Rhône,
in Marseilles.

Alsop buying fish
for dinner.

Alsop sitting on
Le Corbusier: the
Unité d'Habitation
is a building Alsop
has always loved.

Hugh Muirhead,
structural engineer
from Arup and
Partners, at
Marseilles.

200

and admired. So by 1990 Alsop was developing the vocabulary which was to serve his practice into the next century – bold shapes, often circular or oval ('blobs', some called them), an uninhibited use of colour, a desire to give buildings presence (and their users views out) by elevating them on platforms or legs – Alsop likes to compare the art of composition to the act of laying a table.

Already Alsop had demonstrated that his interest lay far beyond buildings as objects in the landscape. His masterplanning exercises, as yet unrealised, posited a rich landscape of forms and ideas, referential and evocative, dynamic and dream like, an idea of the city as a place of delight.

The latter word featured often in his writings and lectures and he saw delight as something which could be found in a railway station or ferry terminal as much as in a museum or private mansion. Alsop's vision of an architecture of pleasure and human fulfilment was already in place and the task was now to bring it to reality.

the new relationship between **ART** and **ARTIST**

do work that allows **THE PUBLIC** to develop its own **VERNACULAR.**

design a range of objects that cannot be related to the name:

IS WHEN THE CONCEPTIC

IN **EXTREMITY** THIS WOULD

NO DEFINITIONS

OF THE DECORATIVE

ONLY BE ACCESSIBLE TO

NO DEFINITIONS

OBJECT

ONE PERSON

MY WORK IS

an **OBJECT** can justify itself **SIMPLY** by being

WITH the client **NOT**

EVENT an **NOT AN O**

FOR

NOT AN OBJECT

BEAUTIFUL

THE CLIENT

THE ESTABLISHMENT

ARCHITECTURE

ART:

NO THEORY

OF RULES HAS BEEN

= **PERFECTING**

NO DOGMA

THE DEATH OF

ARCHITECTURE

REALITY

NO STYLE

ANYTHING THAT IS OBSERVED

building =

AIM:
TO RAISE THE STATUS

IS ALWAYS CHANGED BY THE ● ACT OF

TIME FOR CEREMONIES PARTIES

OF A BUILDING TO A PIECE OF

OBSERVING

RITUALS

ARCHITECTURE

William Alsop OBE RA RIBA FISA BDA AA DIP

Will Alsop belongs to a generation of modern British architects who follow no single school of theory. Observing the practical conclusion of modernist tenets in elegant engineering exercises, he has fought for the assertion of individual creativity in architecture in the belief that it can contribute to the lives of people and communities.

Though an architect of international standing and experience, Alsop forms localised responses in his work which extend beyond the project site to include the canvas of street and town, users, history. This attention centres on personal experience of the brief, the client, and an attempt to draw out aspirations rather than impose solutions. The brief grows organically from debate and experiment, and engenders spontaneous resolutions which materialise into unique structures. The commitment to organism and environment is followed through in a further belief in sustainability; Alsop buildings are implicitly environmentally responsive with low energy service systems.

Will Alsop follows a parallel path as an artist; indeed he feels the two disciplines inseparable. He was a tutor of sculpture at Central St. Martins College of Art & Design, London, for several years, has held many other academic posts, and actively promotes the artistic contribution to built environments; forming collaborations with many artists in different media to this end. Admission of the idea of fluidity and impermanence into both art and architecture have informed his work, confirming his belief that to build is to exercise the eye and the heart rather than the intellect.

206

Further reading

Interview with Alsop in *Regeneration and Renewal* (18 Feb 2001)

Exhibit A, Issue 7 (Sept/Oct 2000)

Master Architect Series III: *Alsop & Störmer* (Images Publishing, Mulgrave, 1999)

'My Kind of Town', *Architecture Today* (April, 1998)

New Urban Environments (Royal Academy of Arts, London, 1998)

David Barrie (ed.): *Power to Change* (BBC Wales, 1995)

Architecture in Process (Academy Editions, London, 1994)

Architectural Drawing Masterclass (Studio Vista, 1994)

William Alsop and Micheal Spens: *Le Grand Bleu, Marseilles: Hôtel du Département des Bouches-du-Rhône* (Academy Editions, London, 1994)

William Alsop and Jan Störmer (eds): *William Alsop and Jan Störmer*, Monograph No. 33 (Academy Editions, London, 1994)

Mel Gooding, (ed.): *William Alsop: Buildings and Projects* (Phaidon Press, London, 1993)

William Alsop, Bruce McLean and Jan Störmer: *City of Objects: Designs on Berlin* (Artemis, London, 1992)

Index

Figures in italics refer to captions

A

AA *see* Architectural Association

Abu Dhabi: breakwater (proposal) 58

Ahrends, Burton & Koralek 99

Archigram 14, 24

Architectural Association (AA) 10, *11*, 14, 26, 31, 62, 67, 178, 197

ArtNet *34*, 64, 67

B

Ball State University, Indiana 55, 58, 67–8, *70*

Barcelona: Realworld project *156*

'Beauty Spot' game *10*, *12*

Behrens, Peter: New Ways 8, *9*

Belfast Kiss *116*

Belfast Urban Park project *77*, 115–16

Billingsgate Pier floating conference centre, London *146*

Birtwhistle installation *10*, 21

Bordeaux: Port de la Lune urban project *162*

Bremen Academy for Art and Music 127, *172*

Bristol: Templemeads Visitor Centre *177*

Butler's Wharf bar and jazz club, London *120*

C

Cairo Conference Centre (model) *87*

Canary Wharf lifting bridge, London 153–4, *167*

Cardiff Bay barrage *169*, 173, 177

Cardiff Bay Visitor Centre 177–9, 180, *188*, *189*, *192*

Chalk, Warren 14, *14*, 21

Chelsea Town Hall, London 72

Cologne: Media Park project 130, *131*, *176*

Compendium Gallery, Birmingham: exhibition (1969) *10*, 16

D

dome (for Shelter exhibition) *11*, 21

E

Eagle Pub (Farringdon, London) conversion *100*, *101*

Earls Barton church, Northamptonshire *9*, 167

Erskine, Ralph: house *9*

F

'Five Young Architects' exhibition (1975) *34*, 64

Floor Bed *14*

'Flying Bedstead' (VTOL aircraft) *8*, 13

Foster, Norman/Foster Associates 13, 14, 68, 154, 189

Fuksas, Massimiliano 130, *132*, 136

G

Groningen, the Netherlands: study for temporary theatre *95*, *114*

Gwent, Wales: art school plan *85*

H

Ham (Roderick) & Partners *62*, 71–2

Hamburg, Germany:

    Bauforum *95*, 124, 127, 188

    Ferry Terminal 127, 130, *146*, *148*

    Hafenstrasse housing project *92*, *95*, 127, *144*, *153*, *169*

    hanging aviary (study) *124*

    Innenstadt Ost *107*, 123–4

    Kunsthalle extension *104*, *105*, 124

    Shipfish complex *106*, *107*, 124

    workshop *173*

Hérouville Saint-Clair, Normandy 130, 136, 138, *154*

    tower *132*, *133*, 136

207

house designs *10*, *34*, *35*, 38, *42*, *54*, *55*, *85*, *86*
Huddersfield Building Society competition (1971) *10*, 38
hydroponics farm design *13*

I
Interaction Centre, Kentish Town, London *26*, *50*, 55, 58,
    115, 173
Island Yard, Docklands, London *147*, *154*

K
Kansas City: study for urban project *118*
Karlsruhe: ZKM *166*

L
Lambeth River Station, London 153, *179*
Le Corbusier: Unité d'Habitation, Marseille 192, *200*
Leeds Corn Exchange project 138, *139*
Lego house *114*
Leuven, Belgium: housing renewal strategies
    (proposed) *47*
London Architecture Club *59*
Lutyens, Edwin: British School, Rome *24*

M
McLean, Bruce *73*, 86, *105*, *107*, 127, 168, *180*
Marseilles, France: L'Hôtel du Département des Bouches-
    du-Rhône *8*, 124, *159*, *177*, 189, 192–3, *196*, 196–7
Melbourne, Australia:
    Docks project *147*, 172–3
    Museum of Contemporary Art *138*, *139*, 172
    Royal Melbourne Institute of Technology *99*
MultiMatch *9*, 34, 86
Murcutt, Glen: Ball House, Sydney *96*

N
National Gallery extension, London 99–100, 123
New Orleans: Fay-do-do structure *78*, *136*
North Greenwich station 180
Northampton County Hall competition 47
Nouvel, Jean 130, *132*, 136
    Tour Sans Fin 99

O
Orlando, Florida: Casino *82*

P
Paris:
    La Défense competition (1982) *88*, *89*, 92, 99
    see also Pompidou Centre
Peckham Library, London 180
Piano, Renzo 24, 86
Pompidou Centre, Paris (project) *15*, 24, 26, 86
Price, Cedric 24, 26, *26*, *27*, 50, 55, 58, 62, 64, 67, 86, 115,
    116, *142*, 180
Project Sink (1970) *10*, *12*, *13*, 21

R
Rainbow Quays housing project, Docklands, London 100,
    136
Realworld projects:
    Barcelona *156*
    Wiltshire *174*
Riverside Studios project, Hammersmith *62*, *63*, *64*, *74*,
    75, 72, 75–6, 86, 92, 123
Rogers, Richard 10, 13, 14, 16, 24, 68, 86
Rome: British School *16*, *21*, *24*, 47

S
St Martin's School of Art, London 14, *26*, *34*, *35*, 62
Seville Expo' 92: British Pavilion proposal *158*, *159*
Shepheard, Paul *59*, 64
Sheringham, Norfolk: Splash swimming pool *115*, *124*,
    139, *139*, 142, *143*, 147–8
Square Mile House *34*
Steidle, Otto 130, *132*, 136
Stonebridge Park community centre 189
Störmer, Jan 123, 189, *200*
Sydney, Australia:
    Darling Harbour cultural theme park project *103*
    ferry stops *96*

T
Tangiers Bay competition (1971) *21*
Taos, New Mexico: housing project *70*, 100
Thamesmead town centre, London *155*
Tottenham Hale station 154, 159, 167–8, *180*

W
West Bromwich: C-Plex project 34, 115, 189
Westminster Pier competition (1980) 72, *73*

Y
York: Theatre Royal 72